When I was a kid I believed everything I was told, everything I read, and every dispatch sent out by my own overheated imagination. This made for more than a few sleepless nights, but it also filled the world I lived in with colors and textures I would not have traded for a lifetime of restful nights.

Stephen King

This book is dedicated to those who have encouraged me to explore the unknown.

I'm forever thankful to Troy Taylor and Lisa Taylor-Horton who have welcomed me into the American Hauntings family as a friend and colleague. Without their faith in the *Haunted Carlinville Tour*, as well as me personally, this book would not be possible.

To Thom, my best friend and partner, who inspired me to reach my goal of completing this book and graciously offers a listening ear to all my ghost stories.

I must also thank my parents, Sonny and Susie Schardan, for their continued support in all aspects of life. Last but not least, I have to thank my Nonni. Even after death she continues to inspire me and offer guidance. She always said my words would get me in trouble, so I guess we'll see if she's right.

HAUNTED CARLINVILLE

History and Hauntings that shaped Macoupin County

KAYLAN SCHARDAN

AN AMERICAN HAUNTINGS INK BOOK

© COPYRIGHT 2018 BY KAYLAN SCHARDAN

All Rights Reserved, including the right to copy or reproduce this book, or portions thereof, in any form, without express permission from the author and publisher.

ORIGINAL COVER ARTWORK DESIGNED BY

© Copyright 2018 by April Slaughter & Troy Taylor

THIS BOOK IS PUBLISHED BY:

American Hauntings Ink
Jacksonville, Illinois | 217.791.7859
Visit us on the Internet at http://www.americanhauntingsink.com

First Edition – September 2018
ISBN: 978-1-7324079-2-3

Printed in the United States of America

TABLE OF CONTENTS

FOREWORD BY TROY TAYLOR - 6

FROM PEASANTS TO PRESIDENTS - 9

LAW AND DISORDER - 26

AROUND THE SQUARE - 47

HERE WE ARE NOW ENTERTAIN US - 80

THIS OLD HAUNTED HOUSE - 90

MACOUPIN COUNTY'S SECRET HELPERS - 107

THE COUNTY CREATURE - 119

MACOUPIN MONEY MAKERS - 124

ALL ROADS LEAD TO BOOZE - 137
Route 66 and Macoupin's Gangsters

MILLION DOLLAR MYSTERY - 153
History and Hauntings of the Macoupin County Courthouse

FOREWORD
BY TROY TAYLOR

I climbed up the stairs to the second floor of the Macoupin County Courthouse and took a look around the corner toward the main doors that entered the courtroom. It was dark – a lot darker than I would have liked when making this trip by myself. I had volunteered to go upstairs and turn on some lights for the guests on our very first *Haunted Carlinville Tour* in the summer of 2015.

I was starting to regret my decision.

I'd been in the Macoupin County Courthouse before – thankfully not for legal reasons – and knew my way around a little bit. We had done some tours and events of the building in years past, but I'd never really wandered around the place much and certainly not by myself, in the dark, listening to every single sound that echoed in the marble-lined hallways.

I don't care how jaded you are about haunted places, the courthouse is an unnerving spot. By the time that I made this lonely trip upstairs, I had been writing about ghosts, hauntings, true crime and the unexplained as a job for more than 25 years. I'd spent the night – sometimes alone – in more haunted houses, hotels, hospitals, prisons, and graveyards than I could easily count. I'd led thousands of people on tours of spirit-infested places all over the country.

So, why was I nervous about walking around an old courthouse? You're going to find the answer to that a little later in this book but trust me when I tell you, I quickly found out what I had to be nervous about.

As I reached the top of the stairs, I walked down the short hall where the two courtroom doors are located and steered myself toward the closest ones. These are very large, very tall, very heavy doors, with gigantic handles on each one. I gave them a tug and they swung outward into the hall. The courtroom was even darker than the hall outside, but I could make out the bench, the rows of seats that lined the room, and the defense and prosecution tables. Kaylan had told me where the light switches were and all I had to do was cross the courtroom to turn them on.

I had plenty of light by which to navigate, thanks to the windows at the front of the building. The light was shining through the doorway that was now behind me. I had opened the massive metal doors up all the way to offer as much illumination as possible.

I had taken only a few steps before I heard a rustle behind me, like something brushed past, followed by a massive, clanging boom! I jumped – and I mean that literally, like a few inches into the air – and spun around because the sound had come from behind me. The two metal doors had slammed shut!

Believe me, I was startled, surprised, and unnerved. But logically, they could have slammed shut for any reason. Was it the wind? But I was on the second floor of a closed-up building. Maybe the floor is sloped. It's an old building, right? But how did they stand open on their own in the first place? Maybe it was a prank that someone decided to play on me. Surely, that was it – except I was in the building alone. There was no one else in the courthouse except for me.

Well, me and the ghosts, that is.

I had no idea if there was another entrance out of the courtroom that would keep me from having to go back through those metal doors but if there was, I was determined to find it.

Thankfully, I found it, and since that time, I have never again been alone in the courtroom of the Macoupin County Courthouse – not at night anyway.

I never knew much about Carlinville or Macoupin County before I met Kaylan Schardan. I knew some of the ghost stories – especially those of the infamous "Million Dollar Courthouse" and once had the chance to stay at the Loomis House, but most of my knowledge about the area was in connection to Route 66 and the old Coliseum Ballroom in Benld. But my friendship with Kaylan has opened my eyes to a wild array of new stories, resident haunts, and restless ghosts. I was as thrilled that she wanted to write this book as I was when she started working with American Hauntings on the *Haunted Carlinville Tour*.

I first met Kaylan when she interviewed my partner, Lisa, and I for a Halloween story when she worked for a local newspaper. I can honesty say that we have been friends – and family – ever since and I don't think that I've ever been prouder of her than when she delivered the finished manuscript for this book.

Within these pages, she has put together a compelling look at not only the ghosts of Carlinville and surrounding Macoupin County, but has also revealed how the ghost stories, legends, and lore have shaped the region's history. This isn't just another book of ghost stories – this is a book about how those stories have become such an indelible part of the area's fabric that they cannot be separated from the mainstream historical events. But this isn't some dry textbook of dates and facts, it's entertaining, fascinating, and, at times, downright spooky.

I hope that you'll be as big of a fan of the book – and of Kaylan – as I am. So, what are you waiting for? Start reading!

Troy Taylor
Summer 2018

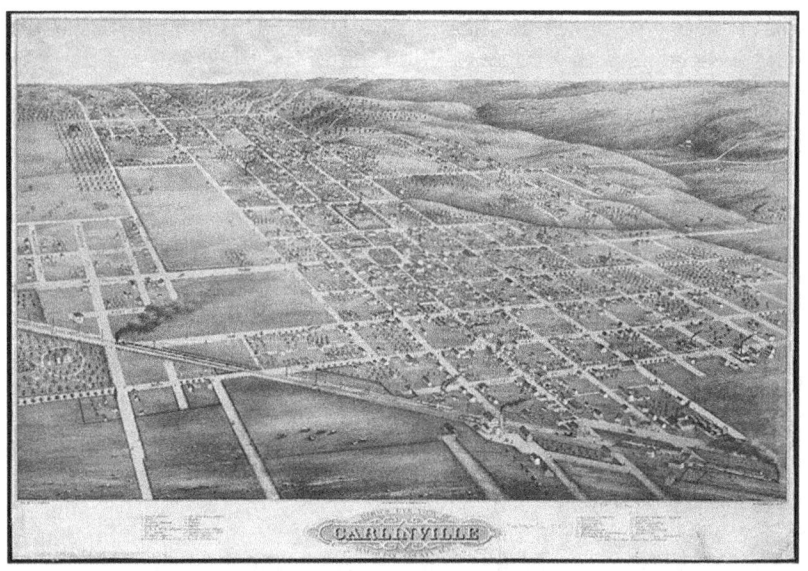

1. FROM PEASANTS TO PRESIDENTS

The town of Carlinville was formed out of exploration, determination, and the desire for community. As part of the "Prairie State", the rural communities in and around Carlinville offered vast farm land, bountiful wilderness, and the opportunity to create a successful settlement. However, with that opportunity came hardships and tragedies that created a unique and sometimes mysterious haunted history.

DANGERS ON THE PRAIRIE

Settlement of the Carlinville area began in 1815 with David Coop and his family. They traveled north from Madison County, Illinois and settled in what became Hilyard Township, several miles south of Carlinville. Roughly 10 years later the family moved to what would become known as "Coop's

Mound" about six miles northeast of town. Shortly after the Coop family came to the area, Seth Hodges and John Love took residence in the area as farmers and began the influx of settlers to the area. In the early days of settlement simply staying alive was a struggle. Disease and wild animals were constant threats. Living in the isolated country miles from the nearest established town meant you acted as your own doctor and your own protector. It wasn't abnormal for children to die of something as simple as the flu or chicken pox. Several cholera epidemics struck the Macoupin County area. One of the most notable occurred in 1851. Dr. Levi Woods was thought of as one of the first infected. Within 12 hours of feeling ill, Dr. Woods passed away. It was said that around 300 people attended the popular doctor's funeral. Shortly after Dr. Woods was buried, those who attended the funeral were struck ill with the disease, many of whom would also die. From that point on, those in Macoupin County made it a priority to isolate the sick and quickly bury the bodies of the dead to avoid further contamination.

Aggressive animals such as wolves, foxes, coyotes, hawks, and other predators made prairie life difficult, especially for livestock farmers. An early settler, William Wilcox, found out firsthand how dangerous the animals could be. After hearing some commotion in one of his chicken coops, Wilcox hurried out of his cabin to see what was going on. When he reached the chicken coop he saw a hungry and determined wolf. He tried to scare the wolf, but the wolf was less than intimidated and attacked Wilcox, tearing into this leg. The settler's dog attempted to aid his owner but was no match for the wolf and suffered a bite. Fighting for his life, Wilcox grabbed the wolf by the throat until the wolf went limp. Wilcox survived the ordeal but was permanently disabled due to the bite and disease carried by the wolf. Sadly, his heroic dog died of his injuries.

The presence of Native Americans was another fear of early settlers. It is believed the Mid-Woodland and Hopewell tribes were likely the ones occupying the land long before anyone else ever stepped foot in the area. The Native Americans relied on the plentiful hunting grounds and resource of the later named Macoupin Creek to provide for their tribes. By the early 1800s, most of the Native American tribes had moved west in search of the bigger game, such as buffalo, which had left the area after some harsh winters in the late 1700s. Even though many of the Native Americans had left the area, settlers still feared their existence. This fear was likely a product of misunderstanding but was also created by the horror stories they would hear, some true and some false.

The settlers did have one nearby account that was likely a motivator for their fear. In the Wood River township, a little over 30 miles south of Carlinville, the unthinkable occurred. On the morning of July 10, 1814, Reason

Reagan made his way to church as he did every Sunday. He left his wife, Rachel Reagan and two children, Elizabeth (age 7) and Timothy (age 3) at the home of Captain Abel Moore who lived about a mile away. There were about eight families in the area and it was customary for women and children to gather at one home when their husbands were away. As an extra precaution against outside danger, block houses were also set up in the area as a place for refuge, one of which was on the Moore's property. The families felt as though they created a safe community. Perhaps it was this feeling of safety that led Rachel Reagan to leave the Moore home for a trip back to her homestead with her children as well as two other children belonging to Abel Moore, William (age 10) and Joel (age 8), and two children of neighbor William Moore, John (age 10) and George (age 3).

CAPTAIN ABEL MOORE AND HIS WIFE MARY.

As night approached William Moore and his wife became increasingly worried that Rachel had not returned with the children. They went to the home of Abel Moore and when they found Rachel and the children were also not there, a group of men assembled, and they began the search along the road to the Reagan home. Abel and William returned empty handed, but William had some startling news. By now it was night time, and while he couldn't be certain, he believed he saw what appeared to be a body lying near the road. He rushed home believing Rachel and the children must have heard an attack and rushed to the block houses for safety. Abel and William, along with Abel's wife and remaining children, set out for William Moore's property and the block house. As they approached William Moore's residence they found his wife Polly, but Rachel Reagan and the children were still missing.

More people had now joined the search party, some on foot and some on horseback, racing through the darkened wilderness towards the block house. While riding on her way through the countryside, Polly Moore came to an abrupt stop. Even in the night she could see a human figure lying near what appeared to be a log. She called out the names of the children and received no reply. With a sinking heart she approached the object, hoping if it was a body they were only sleeping or minimally hurt. She climbed off her horse and reached down towards the shadowy figure only to feel the unskinned flesh of a recently scalped Rachel Reagan. In shock and horror, Polly Moore remounted her horse and quickly made her way home. Once she arrived she immediately put a kettle of water over the fire, prepared to use the scolding water as a weapon for whatever evil may still be lurking out in the wilderness.

The same night as the grisly discovery, a young man named John Harris was sent on horseback to Fort Russell and brought back rangers to the Moore's property. They quickly assembled a group to track the Native Americans they thought responsible for the attack. They followed broken limbs and broken prairie grass on what they believed was the path of the perpetrators. It was reported that they followed the Native Americans north towards modern day Morgan County. A small battled ensued and one Native American was shot and killed. It is said that Rachel Reagan's scalp was found in his belt pouch. Two other Native Americans were said to have escaped and the fate of the others involved remains unknown.

While the battle was brewing up north, the rest of the settlers resumed search for the children. They had hoped they might find the children hiding in the woods, having escaped the brutality experienced by Rachel Reagen. Sadly, that was not the case. The children were found along the dirt road in a mangled condition. All were tomahawked, scalped, and stripped of their clothing. The youngest of Rachel's children, three-year-old Timothy, was found nestled against his mother's lifeless body clinging to life. Blood dripped from his tiny face as he was quickly brought back to the homestead. A message was sent for the nearest physician in Waterloo who did his best to attend to the toddler but unfortunately, he did not survive.

The next morning the small community of Wood River Township prepared three graves. One for Rachel Reagan and her two children, one for Abel Moore's two children, and the last for William Moore's two children. In 1910, Abel Moore's grandchildren erected a monument on Fosterburg Road near the location of the murders which occurred about 300 yards from where Hilltop Auction in Alton stands today. The monument's inscription reads:

In memory of the victims of the Wood Rive Massacre, July 10, 1814. William and Joel, aged eight and eleven years, sons of Capt. Abel Moore; John and George Moore, aged ten and three years, sons of William Moore, Rachel Reagen and her children, Elizabeth and Timothy, aged seven and three years. Murdered by Indians about 300 yards in rear of monument.

The last known local Native American establishment was in the Bunker Hill area and lasted until 1826. Native Americans have preserved their presence around Carlinville leaving behind burial grounds that are located throughout the county, with one located about 1.5 miles west of Coop Mound near the site of the first settlement. The county was even named after the Native American word "Macoupina" which meant "white potato," and was the name given to wild artichoke that grew along the water.

However, Macoupin wasn't always the county name. The area in and around what we now know as Carlinville was at one time considered Madison County and then Greene County, Illinois. It was in 1829 when the legislature propositioned that a new separate county form. Thomas Carlin, an Illinois Senator, and eventual Governor of Illinois, heavily lobbied for the passage of the bill. Some opposed the measure including Peter Cartwright, an outspoken preacher, who felt forming a new county was unnecessary. "God has set apart this region as reservation for the geese and ducks," exclaimed Mr. Cartwright. Even with some opposition, the bill passed. Those geese and ducks would now occupy the county of Macoupin.

THOMAS CARLIN WAS THE SEVENTH GOVERNOR OF ILLINOIS, SERVING FROM 1838-1842.

Thomas Carlin was not forgotten for his assistance in forming Macoupin County and the county seat was named Carlinville in his honor. Despite the obstacles faced by early settlers, Carlinville and Macoupin County continued to grow. In April of 1829, the first commissioners meeting took place in Carlinville and local government started to form.

Land was divided and mapped and Carlinville slowly acquired all the necessities to operate a functional town. Within two years, officials were even able to grant the first divorce in Macoupin County. In 1831, Nancy Sweet filed for divorce from her husband Henry Sweet. At that time, it was uncommon for women to seek a divorce, let alone be granted one. The court determined that Nancy's husband had been absent for two years, leaving her the right to obtain a divorce. The Sweet divorce may have left a bitter taste in

THE CITY HALL LOCATED ON WEST MAIN STREET. THE BUILDING ALSO HOUSED THE LOCAL FIRE DEPARTMENT.

the mouths of judgmental locals, but it marked a new age of law and order in the county.

Even before Carlinville became the Macoupin County seat, it made sure to have a courthouse.

EARLY COURTHOUSES

The first courthouse wasn't nearly as grand as the one that would come to be in 1870. Prior to any courthouse construction, townspeople would offer up their homes to serve as meeting places to conduct official business. This practice grew considerably difficult as the area welcomed additional settlers and a decision was made to construct a courthouse. One of the first appointed commissioners in Carlinville, Seth Hodges, won the contract for the courthouse. For less than $130, the small log courthouse was built. Judges of today are spoiled compared to those who presided in the first courthouse. One door, one window, and one small wooden bench for the judge were the most formal items you would find. The courthouse was also multi-purposed, hosting different churches and town meetings. The commissioners held their first court session in the simple log building on July 17, 1830.

As the county continued to grow, so did the need for a new courthouse. By 1836 plans for a new courthouse were approved by the county. This time around, the citizens were willing to spend a bit more money. Area men,

Harbird and Weatherford, became the authorized builders and were given a $1,500 starting budget. Additional upgrades to this courthouse included a lobby area, fencing, and thankfully, more than one window.

The courthouse quickly became an epicenter for area gossip and entertainment, offering residents an early and personal version of "Law & Order: 19th Century Edition".

Before the Menendez Brothers become "must-see" court drama, there were the Todd brothers. On a cold winter day in 1840, Aaron and William Todd were traveling back to their home state of Indiana with their cousin, Larkin Scott, after a trip out west. Like many young men in the early 1800s, they made the journey out west for a chance at adventure and fortune and when that didn't happen, they decided to head on back home to Mom. On January 26, 1840, they passed through the town of Elm Grove, more commonly known today as the area of North Otter Township near Carlinville. Whether for selfish reasons, evil intentions, or a complete lack of judgment, the brothers began to repeatedly bludgeon their cousin Larkin, leaving him with ghastly wounds and trauma causing his death. They then stole a small sum of money, approximately $26, from Larkin and left the body to be torn apart by area wildlife. They continued their journey home assuming their evil deed would never be discovered, but they were wrong.

THE SECOND COURTHOUSE ON THE CARLINVILLE SQUARE

A few days later, Constable James C. Clark found the body of Larkin Scott and began his investigation into his death. The constable soon discovered the young man was traveling with the Todd brothers and traced them back to Indiana. The Todd brothers were brought back to Carlinville and ultimately charged with the murder of their cousin. The brothers were unable to obtain their own counsel, so area attorneys Frances Hereford, Josiah Fish, John A. Chestnut, and John M. Palmer were assigned to defend them with Attorney David A. Smith representing the State.

The courtroom was filled with those captivated by the violent murder and perplexed by the lack of reasoning behind the act. The trial began on May 5th of 1840 and quickly returned a guilty verdict against Aaron Todd. Within three days of the trial beginning, Judge Brown sentenced Aaron to death by hanging to take place June 2nd between noon and four in the afternoon. He ordered Aaron to be taken within one mile of the court house in Carlinville for his hanging, which was to be completed by the sheriff or his deputy. The verdict for William Todd was far less harsh than that of his brother. William was found guilty of being an accomplice and received two years in prison for his role in the murder.

Due to the popularity of the trial, it was no secret when or where the hanging of Aaron Todd would occur. On the day of the hanging, local newspapers reported that between 5,000 and 8,000 people assembled in the small town of Carlinville to witness the hanging firsthand, bringing their families for a very morbid form of community entertainment. The sheriff realized he had a major problem on his hands. There was no way he could safely transport Aaron Todd outside of town and hold a discrete hanging. If there's one thing Macoupin County people like, it's a good old-fashioned hanging! It was decided that they might as well give the people what they want and decided to assemble a scaffold south of West Main Street.

The sheriff and his men along with Dr. John Logan, a colonel of the Forty-Fourth regiment, were able to assemble approximately five hundred men to preserve law and order while bringing Aaron Todd to his fate. The execution was then carried out with reports stating that Aaron Todd met his death with bravery. The massive crowd of people eventually retreated to their homes and Aaron's body was taken to the cemetery and buried near the back, away from the law-abiding citizens. The story of the sensational murder trial should have ended there but there is a final disturbing epilogue to the story.

A few days after Aaron was buried, someone walking through the cemetery noticed that his grave appeared to be disturbed. Upon investigation, it was discovered that Aaron's body had been exhumed and his head and one of his arms were missing from his body. The mystery remains as to who may have taken the body parts, but perhaps it was one of the thousands who came to his hanging, looking to take a souvenir from the great murder trial of 1840.

HONEST ABE COMES TO TOWN

One of the most notable attorneys to visit Macoupin County's second courthouse was Abraham Lincoln. Over the years I've been told stories of Abraham Lincoln's ghost in Carlinville, specifically that he haunts the Million Dollar Courthouse that is still in operation. Considering President Lincoln died five years prior to that courthouse being built, I find that unlikely. I also can't help but think that he may have more notable places to haunt, like the

White House for instance. Nevertheless, while we might not have Abraham Lincoln's ghost in Carlinville we do have notable Lincoln history.

In 2014, after conducting some research for a newspaper article I was writing, I spoke to a curator from the Abraham Lincoln Presidential Library and Museum who stated the library owns about 1,600 documents with Lincoln's handwriting including two legal documents from Macoupin County court cases. He stated their database of Lincoln documents showed 30 court cases with a Macoupin County connection during the time that Lincoln practiced as an attorney. A large portion of the documents regarding Macoupin County were small bankruptcy cases from 1841-42 and were handled by Abraham Lincoln's law partner Stephen T. Logan.

BEFORE THE PRESIDENT'S BEARD AND TOP HAT DAYS, ABRAHAM LINCOLN WAS A CLEAN-SHAVEN ATTORNEY IN ILLINOIS.

Although the court records with Lincoln's signature may be limited, additional personal correspondence between Lincoln and local citizens did occur. Jefferson L. Dugger, the editor of the *Macoupin Statesmen* newspaper, received a letter from Lincoln on October 29, 1854 regarding an upcoming trip to Carlinville, stating "Do not announce me merely as a compliment to me; I would much prefer saving the labor, unless it promises some good."

One of the more notable Lincoln visits occurred on August 31, 1858 when Lincoln came to Carlinville to deliver a speech vowing for the Illinois Senate seat against Stephen Douglas. According to the *Carlinville Democrat* newspaper, Lincoln stated in part:

"If Douglas can make you believe that slavery is a sacred right...if by special sophisms he can make you believe that no nation except the English are born equal and are entitled to life, liberty, and the pursuit of happiness, upon their own soil, or when they are not constitutionally divested of the God-given rights to enjoy the fruits of their own labor, then may we truly despair of the universality of freedom, or the efficacy of those sacred principles enunciated by our fathers---and give in our adhesion to the perpetuation and unlimited extension of slavery."

The site of Lincoln's speech is in front of the United Methodist Church in Carlinville at the corner of South Broad and East First Streets. A large stone and plaque marks the location.

President Lincoln's ties to the area are also remembered in nearby Bunker Hill. The Lincoln statue in Bunker Hill was donated to the town on September 7, 1904, by Captain Charles Clinton of Company B 1st Missouri Cavalry volunteers. Seven Civil War survivors of Company B were from Macoupin County and were present at the ceremony, including four from Bunker Hill, John Bradenburger, Fred Dabel (Bunker Hill), Jas. G. Rumbolz, E.S. Williams, and three from Carlinville, John Dennison, Jas. Lawrence, and Jas. Pocklington. It is estimated that more than 5,000 people attended the dedication ceremony that was marked with a decorated parade route. The bronze statue of Lincoln sits atop the stone with a woman kneeling at the base. The woman is scribing "with malice towards none."

In more recent years, Carlinville native and award-winning artist David E. Bellm donated original paintings to be displayed around the Carlinville square, including on the outside of the Verticchio & Verticchio law firm office. The painting depicts Abraham Lincoln signing a court document during his time as an attorney with law partner William Herndon. Lincoln is pictured against a backdrop of Carlinville which includes landmarks such as the "Million Dollar Courthouse". Documents from Lincoln and Herndon's law practice are incredibly uncommon. The document depicted in the painting is one of only a few in existence which are signed by both Lincoln and Herndon. This document was filed in the U.S. Circuit Court for the Southern District of Illinois in 1857 concerning Lincoln and Herndon's client, S.C. Davis & Company, a St. Louis based dry-goods wholesaler. The original document has most recently been on sale for $16,000.

Just like every other town in Illinois, Carlinville wants a claim to Lincoln history and there is no question that it as it. Abraham Lincoln spent some of his more formidable years as an attorney attending court cases right on the Carlinville square and future years campaigning on the streets for his political career. Several of Lincoln's friends lived in the area and were called upon for advice during the hardships of the Civil War. Without a doubt Lincoln was familiar with the town and likely the most famous visitor to ever stop by Carlinville.

PRAIRIE SCHOOLS AND SUNDAY SCHOOLS

In the days of early Macoupin County settlement, education was privilege and not a right. Many area children spent little time in school, with most only learning the essentials of reading, writing, and arithmetic before they abandoned education to work on the family farm. However, there were numerous school houses scattered throughout the area. The school houses were primitive, even for the prairie. The buildings were made of unhewn logs with a couple open areas to be used as windows. In many school houses the bare dirt acted as the floor. In winter months, oiled paper was placed over the window openings to keep out the snow. If the students were lucky, a fireplace was installed in the schoolhouse, although it did little to keep out the chilly days of winter.

The first official school in Macoupin County opened in 1824 in the little town of Staunton, just south of Carlinville. William Wilcox acted as teacher, receiving $30 for ten weeks, or roughly $750 today. It seems teachers have always been underpaid. Additional school houses popped up around Macoupin County and towns began to market their school houses as a reason for families to move to Macoupin County.

In the mid-1800s, higher education was becoming more popular and communities began to see the economic value of housing a university. Soon Carlinville would become home to one of the oldest and most unique colleges in Illinois. Blackburn College, a private liberal arts school, is one of eight federally recognized work colleges in the country and the only one with a student run work program. The program allows students to help pay their tuition through on campus employment and has received notoriety for being one of the most affordable private colleges in the country.

The history of Blackburn College starts all the way back before the American Revolution with the birth of Gideon Blackburn in 1772. Gideon was born in Augusta County, Virginia and enjoyed a simple lifestyle with honest Christian parents. He moved to Tennessee in 1787 to live with relatives and shorty after received his calling to the ministry. A couple of years later, Gideon received his preaching license and began a career as a minister.

As the 1800s approached, Gideon became passionate about education and devoted his energy to raising money to establish schools

GIDEON BLACKBURN

for Cherokee Native American children, eventually establishing two schools specifically for Cherokee boys. At first, the schools were a success, but by 1810 both schools closed due to accusations that Gideon was illegally transporting whiskey through the Native American territory. Whether true or not, Gideon and his family decided to move and began their decades of travel around Tennessee and Kentucky where he founded numerous churches and became known for his fundraising skills.

In 1835, Gideon rallied funds to build a seminary in Illinois and by September 1837 a deed was executed to purchase land in Carlinville. Unfortunately, Gideon died in August 1838 and did not see his work completed. After his death the trustees of the property began to sell off portions of the land to pay for the taxes. People began to doubt if any college would ever inhabit Carlinville.

Part of the land purchase agreement Gideon negotiated with the government stated the land would be used for education. Trustees of Illinois College in Jacksonville took notice that the land was going unused and believed they should take over. In fact, the court did give them control in November 1854. However, a month later the decision was reversed, and the Gideon Blackburn trustees were back in control. Realizing the uncertain nature of retaining the land, Macoupin County citizens rallied together to purchase an additional 80 acres for the site of a new educational institution.

In 1855 construction of the college began with the first campus building completed in 1858. Rightfully so, the college was named Blackburn Theological Seminary but eventually expanded to other studies. By 1864 the college offered a full load of courses and allowed women to enroll under the same criteria as men. In 1870 Blackburn College saw their first graduation, with seven students entering the world as Blackburn Alumni with countless others since.

Like many colleges, Blackburn has its own spooky legends to tell and it's easy to understand why. College can be an intimidating and scary place, often becoming the first place we call home besides our childhood bedroom. The walls house hopes, dreams, raging hormones, and sometimes even spirits.

One of the spirits at Blackburn College is said to be Miss Isabel Bothwell. Known as a mentor and friend of Blackburn College, Isabel also became the college's most gracious donor in 1965. Upon her death, the Isabel Bothwell estate left approximately $600,000 to the college, an unusually large sum for a single woman. The money was deemed for the use in the construction and upkeep of a music building on campus as well as the establishment of the Isabel Bothwell Student Loan Fund. Before Isabel's passing she was able to see the preliminary sketches of the building and give her blessing.

AN EARLY DEPICTION OF BLACKBURN COLLEGE

In 1970, the Isabel Bothwell Conservatory of Music was completed with additional space and renovations to come later. Since its completion, Bothwell Auditorium has given music lovers a shiver down their spine that is hard to forget. Students and faculty have reported seeing and hearing doors close on their own, as well as hearing pianos play with nobody around. Some point to Miss Bothwell checking in on her final wishes as the reason for the auditorium's activity.

Bothwell Auditorium has also housed numerous plays and theatre productions. Perhaps it's possible whatever still lingers in this area is drawn to the energy created by the performances. In 2014 a different and less startling supernatural experience occurred when actor Jim Beaver also known as the ghost hunting and demon slaying "Bobby Singer" from the television show Supernatural revived his play Verdigris in the auditorium. As the college's theater program continues to thrive it will be interesting to see if the paranormal activity thrives as well.

Blackburn graduate, Courtney Egner, who I've also had the pleasure of working with on our Carlinville Haunted History tours, documented numerous other unexplained events and locations at the college while writing for the campus newspaper. In the Rahme Learning Center and Renner Art Center people report hearing the shuffling of chairs and footsteps down the hall. Students have even reported hearing someone say "hello" only to find they are alone.

While buildings have a way of creating echoes and the illusion that sound may be closer than it is, the college has seen enough activity that some students refuse to enter portions by themselves. That's the case when it comes to Hudson Hall. Students and faculty have witnessed doors slamming on their own, lights turning on and off, and perhaps even more alarming, growls and inhuman noises that occur beneath the Chapel of the building. It's become so notorious that some students refer to it as "Purgatory."

The Visual Arts Center, a more recent addition to the college in 2003, has also led to an interesting claim. According to a former Blackburn student who was working security in the building in 2012, one regular job was unlocking the doors prior to the start of the day. As he started to walk down a long hallway, he noticed a black figure standing at the end. Rumor says that he was able to take a photo of the apparition, but I have yet to see one emerge. Even so, it adds to yet another building on campus you don't want to visit alone.

Unfortunately, resident halls have not been spared from the paranormal activity. Stoddard Hall, constructed in 1924, is one of the oldest resident halls on campus. Like many of the other haunted areas, those in Stoddard have been known to report hearing unclaimed footsteps, lights turning on and off, and the feeling as though one is being watched. Urban legend over the years has attributed the unexplained in Stoddard Hall to a young man who killed his girlfriend and then committed suicide many years ago, although it doesn't appear history supports that claim.

Butler Hall was completed four years after Stoddard Hall and in recent years has been known as a hotspot for the paranormal on campus. One dorm room, now used for storage, has caught the attention of students. During a Resident Assistant's nightly rounds of checking the dorm they would notice the light to this room turned on. They would then have to unlock the door and turn off the light and the re-lock it before leaving. On their way back through the hallway they noticed that yet again the light was on, but this time the furniture stored in the room was also moved. Knowing they were the only one around with a key made night patrols even more unnerving. Another interesting claim about Butler hall is the feeling the area creates. Students have reported a sense of uneasiness, dread, and despair that occurs specifically in this residence hall.

When you consider the history of Blackburn College, it's not surprising to learn the campus hosts numerous ghost stories. The students may come and go, but the paranormal activity seems to stay the same. Even if they didn't sign up for the course, students may find themselves experiencing a hands-on lesson in the paranormal while attending this historic fixture of Carlinville.

On the prairie, schools and churches go hand-in-hand. Many local schools would double as churches and vice versa in the early days of Macoupin County. When a schoolhouse wasn't available, church service would be held in one of the settler's homes. In the 1800s it was unheard of not to attend some sort of church. Much like today, church was a place where you could catch up on local politics, town gossip, and get a couple minutes of peace and quiet from your children, if you're lucky. Carlinville and surrounding Macoupin County towns have never suffered a shortage of Christian Churches. In fact, most towns, no matter how small, contain at least a couple.

In 1834, the Presbyterian Church became one of the first organized churches in Carlinville. Blackburn College founder Gideon Blackburn was instrumental in gathering interest in the new church and his son Reverend S. E. Blackburn became the first pastor. Within a few years, church officials became disappointed in their congregation's actions and attitude towards services. Church officials openly condemned church members for not keeping the Sabbath day holy. They accused the members of traveling on the Sabbath and engaging in unnecessary social events on a day they believed should be reserved for the Lord. The use of alcohol was also publicly condemned with those in charge vowing to refuse admittance to anyone who would not agree to abstain from alcohol. They even announced their dissatisfaction with the congregation's punctuality and attendance. It shouldn't surprise you that after their airing of grievances, membership dwindled. For those who weren't interested in the Presbyterian church, they had countless others to choose from. Whether you were Baptist, Methodist, Lutheran, or Catholic, there was a church for you.

Over the years, many of Macoupin County's early churches have crumbled and failed to stand the test of time. There is one however that continued to draw a crowd and still stands as a gorgeous historic feature of Carlinville. St. Joseph's Catholic church was formed in 1868. Reverend H. J. Hoven took the lead at the church, which was constructed for $20,000 (over $340,000 today). Within just a few years, the church grew from a congregation of 35 to 120. The church's success allowed it to grow and add

ST. JOSEPH'S CHURCH WHILE IT WAS STILL IN OPERATION

another $20,000 worth of upgrades as well as a parochial school. Over the years the church went through ebbs and flows of membership but stayed consistent for over 100 years.

In the 1990s the church was closed but it would eventually re-open as a restaurant. It was during those years as a restaurant when stories of haunted happenings at the former church were heard around town. Employees of the restaurant would occasionally hear dishes crashing in the kitchen when nobody was in there, or hear the sounds of pots and pans, as if someone was cooking, although the kitchen would be empty. One of the more alarming events involved silverware. Every night the manager would ensure that silverware was properly placed on each table, with the knife, fork, and spoon, all lined up in a row. One morning, she came into the restaurant to find the forks had been moved and placed in a position crossing the knives. Considering nobody else had a key or way to enter the building, and she was positive the silverware was not placed in that arrangement the night before, the manager became a bit startled. The strange movement of the silverware would happen on more than one occasion.

It was a somewhat busy day at the restaurant and out of the corner of their eye, the manager briefly noticed a man in dark clothing sitting at one of the booths. She assumed it was the restaurant owner but when the owner walked through the door she realized it wasn't him. She then looked back at the booth to see who the man truly was only to find he had disappeared. Over the years this man would be seen on several occasions in the exact same booth. As soon as people catch a glimpse, he disappears.

The restaurant has been known to be a family friendly establishment and it was common for children to be seen in the building. One day, a family with a baby was enjoying a meal. The manager was busy running around and tending to daily operations when she almost tripped on a child in the middle of the floor. The child appeared to be between four and six years old with dark colored hair. At the last second, she was able to maneuver her way around the child and when she looked back to make sure he was alright, the child vanished. At first, she assumed the young boy had belonged to the family with the baby but when she approached them she realized he wasn't their child. She looked under the tables and booths and all around the restaurant, but the little boy was nowhere to be seen. Like the man in the booth, he disappeared.

In addition to the apparitions that are seen, the area that was once the church sanctuary has produced some unusual sightings as well. A strange mist has been reported to appear from time to time. During the first sighting of this mist, employees were concerned it may have been smoke but quickly realized it wasn't. As they approached the mist they also determined it wasn't dust, a reflection, or anything they could explain. One woman quickly pulled out her cell phone and captured a video of the mist before it dissipated. It's in this area that people have reported feeling watched by someone or something that can't be seen.

The spirits of the former St. Joseph's church, while active, are also noted for being nonthreatening. Perhaps the man in the booth is a former church member who just likes to sit and people watch as he once did in the old church? Maybe the young boy was a former student at the church's school that was once on the property? Whatever the source may be for the unusual activity, the church still seems alive with spirits even after its closing.

2. LAW AND DISORDER

Creating a town which was safe from the outlaws and criminals was easier said than done, especially in Carlinville's early years. As the town continued to grow not only in citizens but also in industry, the area saw an influx of people trying to make a living, some by illegal means.

A CARAVAN OF CRIME

One of the most unique crime waves in Macoupin County peaked during the late 1800s and early 1900s. Those living in and around the Carlinville area noticed a wave of Eastern European gypsies coming through town. Whether warranted or not, gypsies were often seen as hoodlums and undesirables who brought crime and poverty. These stereotypes and judgements caused gypsies to be persecuted throughout history which led many of them to America. In fact, from 1801-1803, French leader Napoleon Bonaparte transported hundreds of people labeled as gypsies to Louisiana prior to the Louisiana Purchase just to get them out of his country. Unfortunately, the same disdain for gypsies existed in Central Illinois.

The gypsy's unconventional lifestyle of traveling in caravans, fortune telling, and their unusual clothing and beliefs convinced townspeople they were practicing black magic and thievery. Their suspicion deepened when the story of a young woman's abduction reached town.

In 1894, Ella Parse returned home to Mattoon, Illinois to live with her parents. She had recently separated from her husband, Richard Evelin, a man her parents had begged her not to wed. Ella was only 16 years-old when she married Richard. The feisty teen couldn't be dissuaded from marrying the prominent Justice of the Peace and widower. However, she quickly realized that becoming a step-mother to children older than herself was a destiny she could not fulfill. Ella wasn't ready to settle down, and why should she be? She was strong willed, educated, and known for her flawless features. She was simply beautiful. Perhaps, too beautiful.

In the late 1800s, Mattoon became home to a band of gypsies who traded horses, sold clothing, and told fortunes. Many in town despised their presence, but others were fascinated. Like many young women, Ella was curious about the new fashion and fortunes they offered and became a frequent visitor to the camp. Just as quickly as the gypsies rolled into town, they rolled out, leaving in the middle of the night. The next morning as the town realized the gypsies left, the Parse family realized Ella was missing. They called for her around town and stopped every neighbor they could looking for their daughter. The only thing they found was her straw hat. It was trampled near the now abandoned gypsy camp site.

THE YOUNG AND GORGEOUS ELLA PARSE

The Parse family held very different viewpoints about what transpired. Mr. Parse, convinced his strong-willed daughter could never be forced to do anything, believed she had run away with the gypsies. Her mother thought otherwise and believed she was kidnapped. The first sighting of Ella occurred four months after her departure. A woman in Pekin, Illinois who knew Ella Parse's aunt saw a band of gypsies and believed she might have recognized the missing girl. She approached them and asked if anyone there knew of the Parse family. A young woman jumped up and said she did, but just as quickly as she replied she was pulled back into the wagon. The woman saw the young girl struggling and screaming as the horses quickly pulled the wagon away.

About a year after Ella's disappearance, the Parse family received a letter postmarked from Taylorville, Illinois. It was from Ella. It appeared to have been written very quickly with a sense of urgency in every pen stroke. Ella stated that she did not run away, she was kidnapped. She said she was stolen by the gypsy chief who had become infatuated with her. She was unable to break away and every attempt ended with her beaten and threatened with death. Ella pleaded for her father to gather as many men as he could and meet the gypsies at their next camp to rescue her. She told her father to meet them in Carlinville.

Unfortunately traveling to Carlinville became an issue. A strike had occurred on the railroads and travel was only possible by horseback. Mr.

Parse began the excruciating ride to Carlinville, despite continued doubts that his daughter was a runaway and this was some sort of gypsy joke. Once he reached Carlinville he searched high and low for any signs of his daughter. Sadly, the gypsy camp was yet again abandoned and his daughter missing.

Sightings of Ella were reported in Springfield and then again back home in Mattoon where the desperate nature of Ella's condition was undeniable. A woman reported to the Parse family that while the gypsy wagon was traveling through the outskirts of town, Ella had jumped out and raced to her home where she pleaded for help. The woman took Ella inside and quickly hid her as the gypsy wagon approached. As they both held their breath, a loud pounding was heard at the woman's door. Unable to avoid the caravan, the woman opened the door to find a burly vicious looking man named Will Beaton, also known as the gypsy chief. He asked the woman if she saw a young lady near her home. The woman answered "no" but the chief knew she was lying and pulled out a revolver demanding to see Ella. When the woman wouldn't cooperate, he pushed his way through and pulled Ella from her hiding place and ushered her back onto the wagon as they rushed out of town.

Shortly after this frightening ordeal, Mrs. Parse received a post card from her daughter. Yet again Ella pleaded for rescue and said their next camping spot would be Shelbyville. This time Mrs. Parse led the search party. She organized a fresh team and headed out to save her daughter. Upon arrival in

GYPSY WAGON IN THE EARLY 1900s

Shelbyville Mrs. Parse and Marshal Tallman found the gypsy campsite and demanded Ella's release. The chief denied her existence, but the Marshal knew he was lying. By this time Mrs. Parse and law enforcement had assembled a large team and they vowed they weren't leaving without Ella. The chief realized he was outnumbered and would likely pay with his life if he didn't hand over the young woman. Ella was then released to her mother in a reunion full of tears and disbelief as the kidnappers fled off in their caravan. Mrs. Parse could barely recognize her daughter. Ella was thin, pale, and wore rags for clothing, but at least now she was safe.

Ella retold of her kidnapping. On the day of being abducted she went to the gypsy camp to have her fortune read by one of the gypsy fortune tellers. As she was waiting for her reading, someone, presumably the gypsy chief, covered her head with a heavy blanket and quickly picked her up and placed her in the gypsy wagon. She recounted that the chief had become infatuated with her and wanted her for his wife. He forced her into the gypsy lifestyle and even more horrifying, he forced himself on her.

Ella traveled as far as the Dakotas with this group of gypsies and all attempts to escape resulted in assault from the chief both physically and sexually. Even in the arms of her mother, Ella didn't feel safe. In the days following her rescue, Ella continually felt as though she would be kidnapped again. Her parents tried to reassure her the gypsies were scared out of town, but Ella knew better.

One evening while Mrs. Parse was preparing dinner she heard a chilling scream. She peered out the window and saw a gypsy wagon rushing away. Panicked, she rushed to the front door and screamed for her daughter, pleading that her daughter would answer. All she heard was the cold silence.

The neighbor hurried over to the Parse residence and said that she saw a gypsy wagon stop in front of their home. She noticed Ella was standing near the Parse's side door when she was taken by what appeared to be an old woman brandishing a long knife. The neighbor said Ella was then dragged to the wagon against her will. At that moment, the neighbor got a better look at the kidnapper. She was certain it wasn't an old woman after all; it was a man. She could see a beard appearing from the bonnet of the attacker as they pulled Ella into the wagon. The description she gave of the beard and stature of the assailant matched that of the gypsy chief, Will Beaton.

Mrs. Parse immediately set out to find her daughter, but the gypsies yet again disappeared in what appeared to be mere seconds. Mattoon police determined rescue to be almost impossible and search efforts were eventually stopped. Mrs. Parse continued to wait for another postcard from Ella, ready and able to go wherever the gypsies were to save her beautiful daughter once more. Nothing further was said of Ella Parse and if her family ever found her it was kept secret and out of the public.

The uneasiness of gypsy life continued far into the twentieth century. In March of 1931, a young gypsy girl named Bessie was working in Carlinville telling fortunes. One of Bessie's customers accused her of stealing a ruby from her ring during a reading. Bessie was quickly seized by the police and taken to jail. The officers searched Bessie's clothing and possessions for the ruby but found nothing. The police were convinced that Bessie had stolen the ruby and possibly even swallowed it. The woman had almost given up hope that she would retrieve her ruby from Bessie when, according to local reports, the young gypsy produced the ruby from somewhere on her body and gave it back in exchange for release. Wherever Bessie retrieved it from, I would hope they washed their hands after touching it.

In 1950, arrests were made of three gypsy women who were charged with larceny in Carlinville. Their presence in court created quite the spectacle as they appeared in full gypsy regalia. Their attorney L.M. Harlan was able to negotiate a deal where the women would pay restitution and be released. The women were incredibly thankful. In fact, they were so grateful that they initiated a gypsy blessing upon their attorney in court, kissing his hand. They told him that after an hour he could check his billfold and the blessing would be complete. After court concluded and the women left, Attorney Harlan learned the women's blessing had a twist. He was told the women frequently stole from customers by having one of the women sneak money out of their customer's billfold as the others distracted them with the "blessing." It seemed this time it was the attorney who was played for a fool.

Even as late as 1969 a caravan of up to 300 gypsies, this time in luxury vehicles, was located in the town of Medora, about 20 miles south east of Carlinville. Robert Cunningham, a farmer, found the remains of four head of cattle with another Medora man sighting a blood smeared truck leaving town. Macoupin County Sheriff, Elvin Sawyers, believed the gypsies had stolen the cattle and quickly butchered them before heading out of town.

LOCKED UP IN MACOUPIN COUNTY

Gypsies or no gypsies, crime was unavoidable. If it wasn't a gypsy caravan creating trouble, it was cattle rustlers, desperate thieves, or violent degenerates. So, what do you do with all the unfit members of society? You put them in a jail, of course. Macoupin County's first jail was built in Carlinville in 1833 for a total cost of $686. By 1854, it was time for an upgrade and a new jail was built on the southeast corner of the Carlinville square. The second jail consisted of a two-story brick and wood building that

THE MACOUPIN COUNTY "CANNONBALL" JAIL WHILE IT WAS IN OPERATION

unfortunately burned in 1860. The third jail was built right on the same spot. Talk about bad mojo. It didn't last long and eventually, the cells were moved to Alton, Illinois to be used in their prison.

The most notable jail in Macoupin County was the fourth jail, also known as the Cannon Ball Jail. That structure opened in 1869 and remained in operation until 1988 (119 years) with the last prisoners using the same cells built in 1869. The Cannonball jail was designed and constructed by architect E.E. Meyers, the same man who designed the courthouse.

The jail was built using what was called the cannonball method. This unusual building style included placing cannon balls in each joint to prevent any single stone from being removed by the prisoners. This medieval style of the jail was a popular design in the 18th century. It was built to house 17 male prisoners, and one female prisoner, as well as accommodate the jailer and his family in an upstairs apartment. At one time, there were 33 prisoners held at the jail, four which were accused of murder. The jail lacked many modern amenities and conditions were rough to say the least.

Just as far too many ships deemed "unsinkable" end up at the bottom of the ocean, the jail didn't live up to its reputation of being "inescapable." Over the years, numerous inmates snuck out of the jail. Five men even escaped at one time in 1936. Many of the escaped prisoners freed themselves by cutting through the soft steel bars on the windows and then slipping out into the night.

One of the county's most embarrassing escapes occurred in 1968. Two brothers, Charles and James Ray Young were served their dinner at the county jail when the guard forgot to latch and lock the cell door. Seeing an opportunity, the men simply walked out of their cell. After being on the run for several weeks, the men were brought back to Macoupin county to face trial regarding a theft that occurred at an area high school. This time, the guard made sure he locked the cell door.

The jail's reputation for lackluster security took a toll on the county's ego. In the early 1970s, the Illinois Department of Justice became increasingly aggravated with the outdated and unsecure nature of the jail. The *Alton Evening Telegraph* newspaper reported the Department of Justice was threatening to close the jail because "prisoners were walking out of it as if the walls were made of cheese cloth."

After pressure from the Department of Justice, the Macoupin County jail conducted some renovations. Afterwards, local newspapers reported that inmates would be "needing more than a can opener to escape." Even though the cannonball jail is no longer in use, it continues to bring visitors who marvel at the building which reminiscent of a gothic castle.

Macoupin County's jails have their own share of strange and unusual tales. One of the most widely-known prisoners in Macoupin County was a man named Andrew Nash. Mr. Nash's story began on July 4, 1851, when he decided to attend a picnic in Zainesville, Illinois. I think we all can agree that when it comes to Fourth of July celebrations, drinking and partying are almost always a requirement and the same was true in the 1850s.

The party started off rather uneventful. People enjoyed socializing, throwing horseshoes, and, of course, enjoying adult beverages. One of the most popular events of the day was the horse race. Crowds of people gathered to watch the races, including Andrew Nash. During the race, one of the riders, Alexander Lockerman, fell off his horse. Being the polite fellow that he was, Andrew helped Alexander up off the ground. A bruised and embarrassed Alexander didn't appreciate Andrew's gesture. You see, Alexander was known to be a difficult when it came to dealing with other people. In fact, one of the local newspapers reported that Lockerman was of "quarrelsome disposition" or in today's terms, he was a quick-tempered jerk.

After Alexander regained his footing, he pushed Andrew. Of course, Andrew wasn't going to back down from fight and he struck Alexander. The horserace quickly turned into a brawl. By this time, Andrew had been partying for a while and consumed his fair share of booze. Pushing, shoving, and punches were going back and forth between the two men. The fight continued to escalate, until suddenly, Andrew pulled out a knife from his pocket and repeatedly stabbed Alexander in the gut. Alexander fell to the ground, bleeding uncontrollably from his wounds. With blood on his hands and a crowd of people shocked at what had taken place, Andrew immediately ran out of the party – and out of the state. Alexander died a day later from his wounds.

Andrew Nash spent over a year on the run but was eventually captured by police in Arkansas. He was then returned to Macoupin County to face trial for the murder of Alexander Lockerman. Witnesses testified that it was Lockerman who started the fight and even threatened to kill Nash. Andrew's defense relied on the belief that his stabbing of Alexander was in self-defense.

Unfortunately for Andrew, the jury didn't agree. He was convicted of murder and sentenced to hang on May 29, 1854. Andrew's attorney, John M. Palmer, a local man who was very well respected by the community, began trying to overturn the verdict or at the very least try to save the man's life. Attorney Palmer was successful in obtaining a temporary postponement of the execution, moving it to June 23rd. Palmer then obtained written testimony from friends and family of Andrew Nash swearing to his honest character.

Prior to the infamous Fourth of July of 1851, Andrew as known as a popular and law-abiding citizen. Palmer decided to use Andrew's good name to persuade the governor into showing leniency. The letters began to pour into Illinois Governor Matteson's office. The letters from Andrew's friends and family described him as a loving, peaceful, and righteous family man who only acted violently due to excessive alcohol and the threats made by Alexander Lockerman. Countless letters spoke of Andrew's godly character and made convincing pleas for the governor to save his life.

The Lockerman family also sent their own letters to the governor and made their case for the execution of Andrew Nash, even alleging that Andrew's attorney, John Palmer, was coercing the jury members into writing the governor on Andrew's behalf.

On June 23, 1854, the execution date, the governor commuted Andrew Nash's death sentence to life imprisonment. Word began to spread about the governor sparing Andrew's life and while the Nash family and friends celebrated, others became outraged. The Lockermans had already set up camp in Carlinville near the jail waiting for the execution. When they learned Andrew would not be hanged for the murder, they began to form a mob.

The exact number of people who assembled in Carlinville, either rejoicing in Andrew's salvation or enraged by it, was estimated to be 3,000-

4,000. The sheriff's office began to realize they had a problem on their hands. The mob, led by Alexander's brother, Nicholas, was growing by the minute. The furious and vengeful crowd vowed they would see Andrew Nash hang, even if it meant tearing down the jail. The mob continued to grow. Many of its members were drunk and waving weapons in the streets.

The sheriff armed his deputies and 30 volunteers. They vowed to guard the jail and Andrew Nash against the potential invaders. The shouts for the prisoner's death echoed throughout the town, but by 8:00 that night there was no reason to protect Andrew anymore – he was dead. Andrew was found with a bed quilt tied around his neck, with the other end of the bed quilt tied to the rafters of the ceiling. It was an apparent suicide.

However, something didn't quite add up.

It was reported in a local newspaper that there was a "boot" of slack in the quilt. Andrew would have needed to raise his feet off the ground to hang himself. If it was suicide, it wasn't a very efficient or easy way to die. Some alleged the suicide was caused out of desperation. They speculated that Andrew feared the mob would break into the jail and torture him. In that case, he would do the deed himself. Others believed it wasn't suicide at all. According to friends and family, Andrew was full of hope and joy when he heard his life would be spared. He was determined to continue fighting to clear his name and looked forward to seeing his wife and children again.

Rumors that someone broke into the jail and killed Andrew, staging it as a suicide, began to circulate. Some reported that one of the mob members or a member of the Lockerman family killed Andrew. Others said it was an inside job by one of the sheriff's guards who killed Andrew, hoping to stop the madness occurring on the Carlinville streets.

The *Carlinville Statesman* newspaper printed an editorial that expressed remorse over the ugly situation but also printed, "We are proud to say that Carlinville has clean hands in the matter," reporting that it was citizens from out of town that were at the center of the chaos. The town wiped their hands clean of Andrew Nash and the case was closed.

Was it suicide? Was it murder? There was no way to know for sure. What we do know is that the case of Andrew Nash is still open to speculation and some say Andrew still roams the streets of Carlinville. Disembodied

GUESTS OF THE *HAUNTED CARLINVILLE TOUR* LEARNING ABOUT THE OLD JAIL

footsteps and sightings of an eerie shadow resembling a man have been reported around the Carlinville Square on West Main Street. Perhaps these reports belong to the spirit of Andrew Nash who is hoping to put a rest to his mysterious death.

Inmate Martin Fynes also experienced the terrifying nature of Macoupin County's jail. His story even made it into several newspaper publications across the United States. The *St. Louis Globe* and *Nebraska Advertiser* published a story in 1874 that eventually made its way to the *New York Daily Observer*, regarding a medium from Mendota, Illinois, named Betty Milton. Betty became troubled by a spirit she considered evil. The spirit would cause her to speak occasional wild mutterings concerning murder and hatred, but also spoke of remorse. Betty was a respected and well-known medium who was credited with providing connections to those on the other side. In fact, it was common for Betty to host séances and spiritual gatherings to showcase her abilities.

On October 23, Betty held a gathering of approximately a dozen people. Unlike her séances before, this night would change her life. As she sat and mingled with the guests, something, or rather some spirit, entered the room. Betty entered into a trance and became detached from her own personality. Then, out of thin air, an apparition of a tall, slender, young German man with long hair appeared. The spirit then turned to the 12 guests and uttered a supernatural confession:

"I come to make a confession, to express my remorse, to atone as far as I may for a wrong doing. My name, when in life, was Karl Reystadt. On the night of May 8, 1872, I murdered Andrew Garrity. It was my crime for which Martin Fynes died in Alton prison. I was at the time in spirit form but assumed the likeness of Martin Fynes when the deed was done, in order that he might be suspected of the crime and hanged for it. I stole his knife; I purposely encountered two men who knew him, that they might honestly swear to have seen him near the scene of the murder. I hid the bludgeon where it was found. I did all this that I might be revenged upon him for a great wrong he had done me. I was the instrument in the hands of an all-wise justice in taking the life of Andrew Garrity, for he deserved his fate; but my purpose was evil. In my later spirit-life, in higher stages of progression I have learned forgiveness. I have been taught to repent the deeds of my wicked heart. For this reason, I have come back to attest the innocence of Martin Fynes."

(Confession transcribed and printed in the *St. Louis Globe*)

The spirit then disappeared, and Betty woke from her trance. Those present were left speechless and mystified by their encounter that night and sought out further information about the ghostly confession. After researching the names spoken in the spirit's confession it was discovered that both Martin Fynes and Karl Reystadt were once very much alive and had quite the story to tell.

Issues between Martin Fynes and Karl Reystadt began years earlier when the two were working on the Illinois Central Railroad in LaSalle, Illinois. Unfortunately, they both became fond of the same young woman, Ellen Glover. The rivalry for Ellen's affection led to a long-standing feud that was frequently enhanced by alcohol. Eventually, Ellen decided to marry Martin, to the disappointment of Karl. Even though Martin won Ellen's hand in marriage, he never fully trusted his wife when it came to her previous flirtation with Karl. In fact, Martin's hatred for Karl seemed to grow over the years. He took every opportunity to degrade and embarrass Karl, even reading some of Karl's old love letters to Ellen aloud in local saloons. LaSalle was a rough railroad town in those days, where affairs of the heart were not well received. Karl was mocked and degraded after the public reciting of the love letters and decided the best decision would be to leave town.

In 1855, Ellen passed away. Many believed her husband's temper and unfavorable treatment towards her may have led to her death, although there was never a formal investigation. At any rate, Martin decided to move to Carlinville. He began working as a blacksmith with his cousins, the McLaughlins, and began a new chapter of his life. As fate would have it, Martin ran into none other than his old enemy, Karl Reystadt. The two foes must have thought alike because Karl had also decided to start his new life in Carlinville. Karl had even opened a saloon in town.

It didn't take long for Martin to start back where he left off in LaSalle -- tormenting and bullying Karl. Again, he mocked Karl's failed attempts at love and took every chance he could to humiliate the poor man. Finally mustering up the courage, Karl decided to stand up for himself and confronted Martin. He was no match for this adversary. Karl was beaten badly, humiliated by Martin once again. Karl simply couldn't take it any longer. It seemed no matter where he went, or how much time had passed, Martin was there to torment him and make his life hell. There was only one way out -- death.

Shortly after his most recent humiliation, Karl crawled into bed. He was distraught, beaten, and broken. He took his own life by swallowing poison. A note was found next to the bed that admitted his suicide but blamed Martin for his death, vowing to be a burden to him in death as Martin had been to him in life.

Needless to say, Martin didn't mourn Karl's death. He continued life as usual, drinking, and causing trouble wherever he could. Martin's lifestyle led him to lose his blacksmithing business. Still, Martin had a way of landing on his feet and in the spring of 1862, he decided to go into business with an Irishman named Andrew Garrity, selling horses and mules in the St. Louis area. Martin was given the task of taking the livestock to St. Louis, but things went badly. When he returned to Carlinville, he told Garrity that the $5,000 he received as payment had been stolen. Garrity didn't believe the sensational story and Martin was arrested and indicted for embezzlement and fraud. However, Martin wasn't behind bars long. He quickly made bail.

A few days after Martin's release, Garrity was found dead on the side of the road with a crushed skull and several stab wounds to his back. Near the body, a bloodied club was found, along with a bowie-knife that was known to belong to Martin. It didn't take long for Martin to be arrested again, this time for the murder of Andrew Garrity. The trial was filled with conflicting reports concerning the night Garrity was killed. Two men testified they saw Martin near the location where the body was found and that he was holding what appeared to be a club. They stated that they tried to talk to Martin, but he didn't respond. It almost appeared as though he was under some sort of spell. Four other men testified they were with Martin on the night of Garrity's death and provided him with an alibi.

The only thing that could not be disputed was the knife. There was no question that the knife found at the scene of the crime was in fact Martin's. The conflicting testimony led to two mistrials.

While waiting for a conclusion to his legal saga, Martin spent some time at the Macoupin County Jail. During his time in jail, he claimed he was visited by the spirit of a young, tall, and slender man with German features. He said the spirit would constantly torment him and make claims that he would meet his death by hanging. Martin was terrified. People assumed Martin was either crazy or trying to gain sympathy and dismissed his claims. That was until one of the guards witnessed something he would never forget. The guard removed Martin's cell mate and upon return to the cell saw an apparition standing next to Martin. The guard was astonished. The apparition looked exactly like Martin, differing in no visible way.

The officer was so frightened at this vision that he quickly closed the door and called for help. A few minutes later, the guard returned but the spirit had disappeared, and Martin was found on his pallet in a state of trance. The guard's report of any supernatural occurrences was dismissed. Many believed the guard was either sleep deprived -- or crazy like Martin.

Up until his death, Martin believed the murder of Andrew Garrity had been committed by that young, tall, slender demon with German features who visited him at night. Was Martin's "demon" really the spirit of Karl Reystadt? Was Karl keeping his promise to obtain revenge on the man who brought him so much heartache and misery? Whatever the case, Martin Fynes never faced his third trial. He was transported to an Alton, Illinois prison where he died alone in a state of complete and utter terror.

TELL THE TRUTH AND SHAME "THE DEVIL"

We all know people who seem to be born into a privileged life. Good looks, good luck, and charm seem to always steer them towards the finer things in life. Lester Kahl was one of these people. Lester came from a wealthy family in Shipman, Illinois. His father, Edward Kahl, operated a farm supply store and even became a deputy sheriff. Edward Kahl was one of the most well-respected men in the county. His son, Lester, knew how to ride the coat-tails of his family's good name. He never put much work into his school lessons and he didn't care to join in any sports or youth groups. Lester would rather do things his own way.

After numerous years of struggling through school, Lester left academics behind at age 18 without achieving his high school diploma. The lack of education didn't bother the young man and, why would it? His family had money, influence, plus he was busy with other extracurricular activities, many of which included the young ladies in the area.

Lester's parents tried furiously to persuade their son to go back to school but his spoiled and independent nature wouldn't hear reason. Determined to live his own life, on his own terms, Lester packed his bags and traveled to Pike County, Illinois, where he worked shucking corn. His taste of adulthood didn't last long. After just a couple of weeks, Lester became sick and returned home to Shipman where he worked odd jobs and entertained ladies with his good looks.

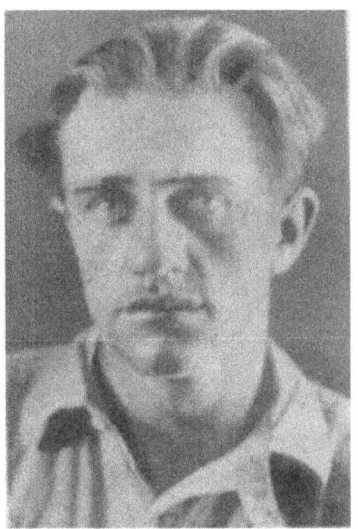

LESTER KAHL

One of the young ladies who caught his eye was Ruby Calvert of Medora, a nearby town with more farm animals than people. The two married in October of 1919 and with the financial help of his parents, moved to East St. Louis. Lester was determined to prove his parents wrong. He wanted to show he could be a responsible adult and that all the worry and the lectures given by his parents were wrong.

Like his ego, Lester's dreams were big. He started working at a meat-packing factory and had his mind made up that he would be opening his own business in no time. Unfortunately for Lester and his bride, there was one problem -- Lester didn't like authority and his temper would often get the better of him. Lester left that job and decided to take up electric work. History repeated itself and Lester was again unemployed.

The couple moved back to Macoupin County and Ruby's parents invited them to stay in Medora where the family owned a jewelry shop. It didn't take long for Ruby's father, Andrew, to realize something was wrong with his new son-in-law. One day, he walked into the jewelry workshop to find Lester sharpening a menacing looking knife. He asked Lester, "What are you doing?" Lester replied that he was "going hunting." Andrew shook his head and went about his business. He returned to the workshop about an hour later and found Lester still sharpening the same knife. "Surely, it's sharp enough now Lester," Andrew said, baffled at the sight of his son-in-law.

"I have to get it sharp if I'm going to get $500 from my father," Lester replied as he held out the piercing knife stabbing the air.

Andrew was shocked and frightened at Lester's reply. Suddenly, Lester began to laugh -- laughing in a way that made Andrew's hair stand on end. What a horrible joke, thought Andrew, but perhaps the boy had a sick sense of humor.

Things became even more worrisome when one evening Andrew came home and found everyone upset and in tears. Earlier in the afternoon, Lester was trying to round up one of the horses. It was playing in the field and everyone was enjoying seeing it frolic and prance around – well, everyone except Lester. Lester went into a rage and grabbed his shotgun. He ran out into the field and shot the poor animal in the head. Andrew was furious and shocked at the young man's behavior. He could no longer ignore that something was undoubtably wrong with his son-in-law.

Andrew brought Ruby aside and sat her down for a heart-to-heart talk. Breaking down in tears, with her hands covering her face, Ruby admitted that Lester was unfaithful to her in St. Louis and had now been unfaithful in Medora. Worse than that, he had a temper and would repeatedly slap and hit her during fits of rage. She simply didn't know what to do.

Andrew confronted Lester about Ruby's confessions. Lester went into a rage, but Andrew wasn't going to back down. The yelling and threats continued into the night and ended with Lester storming out of the house, vowing he didn't want to be married anyway. The Calverts breathed a sigh of relief and Lester was again free to live the life of a playboy.

For the next two years, Lester went from one job to another, using his parent's money to live a rather luxurious lifestyle. Being a good-looking, charming, and somewhat wealthy young man afforded Lester many pleasures, most notably the pleasures of women. He was known to flash his money around and date numerous girls at one time, which earned him the nickname, "The Devil" because he was so impish with the ladies and could persuade them to do whatever he wanted.

One night, Lester agreed to go on a double-date with one of his friends. He was warned that the young women were "good girls." Typically going on dates with girls that had self-respect would have been considered a waste of time for Lester, but he gave in to his friend's request and agreed to the date. Lester's companion for the night was a beautiful, raven-haired young woman by the name of Marguerite Slaughter. Marguerite was the daughter of George and Alice Slaughter of Gillespie. Her father was a miner and her family was well-respected. This was not the type of girl that Lester usually courted.

Upon seeing Marguerite, known as one of the prettiest girls in Gillespie, Lester decided to try something different. He would try to be a gentleman. The two enjoyed a nice evening of dancing and partying. When it was time to say goodnight, Lester didn't even dive in for a kiss but instead thanked the young woman for a wonderful evening. Marguerite was impressed and quickly fell head-over-heels for Lester.

Lester decided to give this new gentleman persona a try. He had enjoyed his time with Marguerite, he mused, perhaps it was time to grow up. The truth was, Lester began to fall in love with the "good girl" he would have previously ignored. The two dated for several weeks and the love continued to grow.

MARGUERITE SLAUGHTER

The relationship hit a speed bump when, during one of their dates, Lester took Marguerite to a dance. At the dance he introduced her to some of his friends. One of the friends referred to her as "The Devil's new girl" and when Marguerite asked what he meant by that, the man spilled Lester's secret love of fast women with less than pure reputations. Marguerite was devastated. As the date ended, Marguerite asked if the nickname was true. Lester admitted it was but professed his love for her and swore he changed his ways. Marguerite didn't buy what Lester was selling and she ended the relationship.

Typically, Lester would simply move on to another girl, but this time was different. He couldn't get Marguerite out of his head and he begged her to see him once more. Luckily for Lester, Marguerite was missing him, too, and they agreed to talk. The two met and quickly, all was forgotten. As the two embraced, Lester swore his love for Marguerite and, to ensure her trust once more, he asked her to marry him. Charmed by his handsome smile and longing for love, she agreed.

In September 1924, Lester and Marguerite were married in Litchfield, Illinois. After the wedding, the two returned to the Kahl family farm in Shipman. The Kahl family was impressed with their new daughter-in-law and leased some farm land to the couple, agreeing to help them financially until they could yield a crop and profit. Along with their money, they gave Lester a bit of advice -- keep his past a secret and start anew with Marguerite.

Wedded bliss didn't last long for the couple. Within a couple of weeks of moving to the farm, one of Lester's dirty little secrets reached his wife. Marguerite learned that her husband was married before. She confronted him at dinner, "Is it true Lester, is it true that you were married before me?" Marguerite asked with tears streaming down her face.

Lester flew into a rage and wrapped his hands around his wife's throat. She gasped for air and as the tears continued to pour from her eyes, Lester seemed to suddenly snap out of it and released his grip.

Marguerite sat back in the chair, shocked and frightened. Lester calmed himself and admitted to the marriage but stated he had received a divorce. He returned to the field and began to worry about the status of his marriage. You see, Lester lied to his wife -- he hadn't received a divorce from his first wife, Ruby, and by marrying Marguerite he had committed bigamy. Lester was a sly man and had been able to keep the secret under wraps, until now. Would Marguerite leave him? Would she find out he was still married and turn him into the police? He knew he could lose it all, most importantly, the land and money his parents had given him.

When Lester returned home he realized he could perhaps convince his young wife to stay quiet. It didn't' take long for Lester to charm his way back into Marguerite's heart. They expressed their affection for one another and Lester assured her their love would get them through anything. As they embraced, something sparked Marguerite to pull away from Lester and she went outside to sit by herself. After an hour or so, she returned and admitted that while she loved him, she wanted to go back to her parent's house in Gillespie until Lester could prove he was truly divorced. She didn't want her parents to hear about Lester's past affairs from town gossip and knew she needed to tell them before anyone else could. The couple spent that night with their backs facing each other as Marguerite cried herself to sleep and Lester lay wide awake.

The next morning Marguerite wrote her father asking him to come get her, agreeing with Lester that Saturday, a few days away, she would return to Gillespie. The time leading up to Marguerite's return home was tense and filled with tears throughout the day, but, to the outside world, the couple seemed happily married.

On September 20, the Thursday before Marguerite was scheduled to leave Shipman, Lester asked her to meet him out in the field at around noon to scare up some doves for supper. Still acting as the dutiful and loving wife, Marguerite agreed. She walked up to the wagon where her husband was standing. He directed her to go on the other side of the wagon. Marguerite walked over to the other side and as she turned back toward her husband, Lester picked up a 10-gauge shotgun and fired, striking Marguerite in the left shoulder and cheek.

Marguerite fell to the ground, landing on her back. Lester stood over his lover and, as she laid their bleeding in the field, she looked up and said, "Well...you have done a good job of it" she then gently sighed and asked, "Why did you do this to me?" Lester replied by raising the shotgun and firing again.

Lester then picked up his wife's lifeless body and wrapped it in a horse blanket before placing it in the wagon. He drove around the farm and finally found a spot about a half-mile away, where he dug a knee-deep grave and placed the young lady's body inside. Lester continued with his day as though nothing had happened. When supper time came, he decided to go to the Jasper family homestead nearby, where he asked to stay the night. He said his wife had decided to hitch a ride to Gillespie with some people and he was rather lonely.

Was it a guilty conscience that made Lester fearful of being alone? More likely Lester was setting up a story to explain his wife's disappearance.

Luckily for Lester, the Jasper family mentioned that they saw a young woman get into a vehicle earlier in the day and figured it must have been Marguerite. The girl that Jaspers saw was likely one of Kahl sisters getting a ride from their father, but they didn't know the difference and obviously, Lester wasn't going to correct them.

The next day Lester went about his business and as he was working out in the field he noticed a car drive up. It was Mr. and Mrs. Slaughter. This was the moment of truth for Lester. He mustered up some courage and took a deep breath. Lester walked over to the car and immediately asked where Marguerite was. The Slaughters were confused. They were here to pick Marguerite up, why would she be with them? Lester gave quite a performance. He told a story about how Marguerite had left with some people the day before and was on her way to Gillespie. The Slaughters began to panic. Where was Marguerite?

The Slaughters and Lester then decided to travel to Carlinville and file a report. Lester's father was still a deputy sheriff at the time and the girl's disappearance was given the utmost importance. Soon after arriving at the sheriff's office, it became obvious that Lester was incredibly nervous. Lester sat there fidgeting and avoiding eye contact as the officers began to question him. He stated that around 8:00 p.m. the evening before, a car pulled up to their house and a young woman began to speak to Marguerite, who then asked Lester if she could go to her parents' house. He didn't know the people in the car but for some reason, agreed to let her go. He went as far as to say that he hitched a ride with them to the local store where he bought some grocery items and then walked back to his house. As the questioning continued, Lester grew even more agitated. When pressured, he would give a few more details, such as the woman in the car being named "Mary" and some young man in the back having "long sideburns," but still he claimed he had no idea who the people were. His story was odd to say the least.

The search for Marguerite began. The police searched for the mysterious Ford Coupe that Lester mentioned as the car that picked up his wife. Lester must have realized that his story wasn't being believed by everyone at the sheriff's office because that next Tuesday, he returned to Carlinville and gave another detail to help steer blame away from himself. He stated that he recently found out Marguerite was having a relationship with a young man in Gillespie. Lester remarked that she must have ran off to be with her lover.

The Slaughters could never believe such scandal about their daughter. Still, the Kahls were a good family and even though Lester's story didn't seem to make sense, they weren't going to arrest a deputy's son without good reason. Days passed and there was no sign of the young girl.

Unfortunately for Lester, secrets have a way of catching up with you. A wife of one of the area deputies was chatting with a friend when the subject of Ruby Calvert came up. Remember Ruby? She was Lester's first wife. The sheriff's department decided to pay Ruby a visit and that's where they learned of Lester's abusive past and the fact that he was still married to the young Medora woman.

That night, Lester was arrested on bigamy charges, which was the very thing he was trying to avoid. Lester's own father, Deputy Sheriff Edward Kahl, brought him into the county jail and as his father had done so many times before, he bailed his son out of trouble by paying the large sum of $2,000. Yet again, Lester was protected by his family's good name and money.

The sheriff's department was conflicted. They heard from the Calverts about Lester's violent tendencies and they knew Marguerite was not the type of girl to just run away. They didn't trust Lester and they didn't believe him but still, they had to tread lightly when dealing with the son of one of their own law enforcement brothers.

Even so, Lester's luck was running out. The sheriff's department decided it was now or never. Late that night, Lester was arrested for murder and brought to the Macoupin County Jail in Carlinville. Hour after hour, the officers questioned Lester, but he didn't break. Lester was a smug young man who had never faced consequences in his life. Why would he start now?

The officers were getting nowhere but then remarked they were going to search the Kahl family farm. Lester turned white and suddenly, the confidence disappeared from his face. Lester panicked. He jumped up and professed that Marguerite killed herself and he buried her body on the farm to hide the shame of her suicide. He stated that Marguerite was an insecure girl who accused him of cheating and out of grief, shot herself.

The officers knew suicide was not how the young lady met her demise but at least they had Lester sweating. Lester was taken to the farm where he led the officers to Marguerite's grave. As they unwrapped the horse blanket to reveal the young bride, Lester refused to look. For once in his life, Lester was cowering and could no longer charm his way out of trouble.

Lester was indicted on murder charges on October 15, 1924 and plead not guilty. The Kahl family couldn't seem to come to terms with Luther's guilt and spent a small fortune to hire Springfield Defense Attorney, Edward C. Knotts. If nothing else, the Kahls wanted to see their son die a natural death, even if it was behind bars.

Lester's trial took place in the Macoupin County Courthouse and, as one can imagine, it was sensational. The Kahl trial became the biggest scandal of 1924 -- a young beautiful couple from two of Macoupin County's most respected families ended in tragedy at the hand of the handsome and charming groom. It was must-see courtroom drama.

State's Attorney L. M. Harlan had a solid case against Lester and Judge Frank Burton was not the type to tolerate nonsense or excuses. Still, Lester's attorney put on the best defense possible He argued his client was under the influence of alcohol at the time of the shooting and was unaware of his actions.

On November 28, likely seeing that his trial was not going to end in his favor, Lester threw himself on the mercy of the court and plead guilty. The next day, Judge Burton sentenced Lester to death. Attorney Knotts sought a new trial but was denied and the hanging was set for December.

A petition circulated throughout Carlinville asking Governor Len Small to postpone the hanging until after Christmas, so as to not ruin the holidays for the townspeople. Mrs. George Thomas Palmer, President of the Illinois Federation of Woman's Clubs, urged the Governor to deny the request. An advocate for woman's rights and ending domestic violence, she wrote, "I believe the great majority of Illinois women join in this plea that no reprieve, postponement, or commutation of sentence be allowed. If he is hanged as he deserves, I believe it will be a determent to other criminally inclined persons." The Governor listened, and the request was denied. Christmas or not, Lester was going to hang.

Deputy Sheriff Edward Kahl, who for decades looked the other way at his son's indiscretions, could no longer avoid the truth, "Let the law take its course. I tried to do the right thing for him and failed...I wash my hands of him for good...." The family's good name was now forever tarnished.

On December 22, 1924, 24-year-old Lester Kahl was led to the bull pen at the Macoupin County Jail. It was around 8:15 a.m. when Lester walked outside and was greeted by about 500 area citizens who assembled to see the young man hang.

True to his ego, Lester appeared stoic and almost relaxed as he walked towards his death. He was dressed in his Sunday best with a white carnation attached to his coat. As he approached the hangman, he let out an eerie laugh. He then turned to the crowd and stated, "People, I am sorry for my sins and I have prayed to God to forgive me. I am unafraid, and I am happy."

A white cloth was fitted over his head and Kahl was led to the noose. He stepped forward and the noose was tightened. Lester hung for 15 minutes and was then pronounced dead. It was the last hanging in Macoupin County and the husband in one of the shortest-lived marriages, lasting only 3 weeks before he murdered his young bride.

During American Hauntings' 2017 Dead of Winter Festival in Carlinville, I gave a presentation on Carlinville history and included the story of Lester Kahl. After the presentation, one of the guests stopped me. He said that he knew the current owners of the Kahl property and had heard stories of a spirit that wanders the field. The apparition is said to appear confused and lost.

He didn't give the ghostly sightings any thought until he heard the story of Marguerite Slaughter's death. He seems to think it is the young bride who is haunting the Kahl field, making sure she is not forgotten. Every now and then, I go to visit Marguerite's grave in Gillespie so, at least during those visits, the young raven-haired girl is remembered.

3. AROUND THE SQUARE

Throughout Carlinville's growth, there has been one area of town that has prospered above the rest. It is known as "The Square." This center roundabout is a unique feature that sets the town apart from others in Macoupin County. Carlinville laid the first bricks around the square in 1892 at a cost of $13,851. They continued to expand the brick roads to West Main Street, South Broad Street, North Broad Street, and East Main. By 1900, the town had spent over $56,000 (almost $1.5 million today) on brick streets. It was a hefty price to pay but it earned the town some notoriety in 1926 with the arrival of Route 66.

CHECK INN TIME
CARLINVILLE'S HISTORIC AND HAUNTED HOTELS

Hotels have a reputation of being some of the most haunted locations you'll find. If you think about it, their haunted reputation makes sense. Imagine how many people have come and gone from every hotel room...some

EARLY 1900S PHOTO OF THE CARLINVILLE SQUARE

are families, some are friends, and others are lovers. Virtually every emotion was likely experienced in a single hotel room. Feelings of joy, excitement, and lust, along with disappointment, loneliness, and heartbreak are embedded in the walls.

On second thought, maybe you shouldn't think about it too much.

The idea of a hotel is off-putting in and of itself. You're staying in a strange room with a strange bed, likely in a strange town. The media has fed into this uneasiness and commonly uses hotels for settings of horror, including classic movies such as *The Shining* and television shows like *American Horror Story*. While many tales of hotel horror are works of fiction, some are reality.

Carlinville has its own rich history with hotels, with the first known inn popping up in the 1830s. In 1834, Jefferson Weatherford purchased 80 acres of land slightly south of Carlinville for $1.25 per acre. The next year, he built a modest stagecoach inn on the property, which was located about three miles southeast of Carlinville along the current Route 4. The inn was then sold to Tristram P. Hoxey, making Jefferson Weatherford a fine profit.

The building became known as Hoxey's Inn and as people began to arrive in the area, they created a nice little settlement that was dubbed "Weatherford's Prairie."

Hoxey's Inn was located near a Native American and stagecoach trail, which made it a popular stop for travelers. In fact, it is said that Abraham Lincoln stopped by the inn on at least one occasion.

The inn was constructed of oak logs about 20-feet long, using wooden pegs and notches to fit the logs together to form the building.

OVERGROWN WEEDS KEEP HOXEY'S INN HIDDEN, BUT IF YOU KNOW WHERE YOU TO LOOK, YOU CAN STILL FIND IT

Unlike most structures in the early 1800s, the inn was two-stories. The first floor had four rooms, two of which were the kitchen and dining areas, which were painted in homemade lime whitewash. The glassless windows provided little protection from wind and weather, however, a mixture of soil, horsehair, and wood is said to have been used to create a type of insulation. A wooden ladder led patrons upstairs to the men and women's bedrooms. Fireplaces did exist for cooking and heating purposes but overall the inn was incredibly simple and primitive.

Eventually, "Weatherford's Prairie" was deserted. The trail became less traveled and people began to move into the city. Little remains of the vanished settlement, although if you were to explore closely, you will likely find remnants of old foundations near the inn's location.

Even though the settlement didn't last, the men responsible for its start, Jefferson Weatherford and Tristam Hoxey, both became widely respected Macoupin County men. Tristram became the county recorder and clerk and Jefferson became the county sheriff and eventually served as Texas State Senator in the 1860s. Jefferson Weatherford even has the Texas town of Weatherford named after him.

The Fieker family eventually purchased the property and kept it in the family for over 130 years, even using the inn as the family home. When they sold the land in 1998, they worked tirelessly to dismantle the building to move it to a new location. They numbered each log and carefully reconstructed it at the intersection of Broad and Blackburn Street in Carlinville. A metal shell was placed over the re-built Hoxey's Inn to preserve it for as long as possible, allowing it to be visible by visitors who wish to see the historic structure.

Additional hotels popped up in the Carlinville area, especially during the early twentieth century. These hotels included the Rouland Hotel on West Main Street and the Malcor Hotel on the southeast corner of the town square. Despite the abundance of hotels that have operated in Carlinville over the years, there is one that

ROULAND HOTEL IN CARLINVILLE

stands out amongst all of them. In fact, it's still a fixture of the Carlinville square. The Loomis House Hotel is known as one of the grandest -- and most haunted -- buildings in town.

In order to fully understand the hotel's legacy, I think it's important to understand the man behind the building: Thaddeus L. Loomis. We might as well start his story at the very beginning.

The Loomis family's history in the United States began with Joseph Loomis. He was one of the first settlers in Windsor, Connecticut, when he immigrated to America in 1638 from Essex, England. He made his living as a draper and lived a modest, well-respected life. Fast forward almost 200 years and a new Loomis was making history.

George Washington Loomis, a fourth great-grandson to Joseph Loomis, soiled the Loomis name for generations to come. George Washington Loomis and his wife, Rhoda Marie Mallet, who was described as a gorgeous woman with a fiery temper, moved to an area dubbed "Nine Mile Swamp" in Madison County, New York in 1802. Rhoda was known to be a little rough around the edges and seemed to take after her father. Rhoda's father was an officer during the French Revolution, who proudly embezzled money from the French crown. It didn't take long for the couple to turn to the life of crime themselves, beginning with petty theft that quickly escalated. The parents taught their thieving ways to their 12 children, especially George Washington Loomis Jr.

Their sons quickly graduated to livestock rustling and burglaries and they sold the stolen goods for a hefty profit. They also began counterfeiting money and using that money to pay off witnesses and law enforcement. Anyone who dared cross them would find themselves beaten to a pulp or their home mysteriously burned to the ground. There is no doubt the Loomis family had developed a criminal enterprise.

In 1849, the Loomis family faced a narrow escape. Officials had conducted a raid on the Loomis property and found a variety of stolen goods. Luckily for them, all charges were dropped due to a lack of proof regarding who owned the items. Still, the family realized they needed to take extra precautions and for George Washington Jr., it was a sign he should move away for a while, heading out west in search of his fortune.

George, Jr. soon returned home and realized he had struck gold in another way -- the Civil War. The war offered ample opportunity for the Loomis gang to regroup and use the troubling times in their favor. They began stealing horses and supplies that they would sell to the Union Army. As rations became scarce, the gang amped up their thieving ways and even started stealing back the horses they sold to the Union Army and then selling them back to the desperate soldiers. They were shameless when it came to their actions.

By 1865, the tolerance for the Loomis gang had come to an end. Not even threats of violent or fire could stop a group of men, many of them Union Soldiers who were particularly disgruntled over the Loomis ways, from attacking the family farm and ultimately killing George, Jr. The family gang was soon dismantled, especially after another attack in 1866 that saw the family homestead burned to the ground. Those who were left in the Loomis family tried to steer clear of the negative history associated with their name and many began to migrate out west.

Today, it is said that George Washington Loomis still haunts the grounds of the family home. Legend says Loomis threatens a violent death to anyone who tries to own the land once belonging to his family and curses anyone disgracing their name. The Loomis' became one of the first widely recognized family gangs in the United States, long before the Irish or Italian mob families rose to power.

LOOMIS GANG MEMBERS WOULD BECOME FREQUENT FEATURES ON AREA WANTED POSTERS

Horace Loomis, a law-abiding cousin, left New York and the tarnished family name behind in 1838 when he moved his family to Carlinville. He arrived with his wife, Julia Tuttles, and three sons, Thaddeus, William, and Horace Julius. They raised their children as honest young men -- or tried to anyway.

The most promising son seemed to be the oldest, Thaddeus Levi Loomis. He was about 12-years-old when his family came to Illinois. He was known to be a hard worker and quick study. Unlike most of his classmates, Thaddeus continued his education at Illinois College in Jacksonville and then went on to the University of Kentucky, where he pursued a law degree. He graduated in March 1849 as an accomplished law student.

After his education was complete, Thaddeus began looking for something a bit more exciting in his life. After contracting a touch of "gold

THADDEUS LOOMIS

fever," he decided to assemble a group of eight men with mules, wagons, rations, and a ton of courage to make his way out west to California in search of a golden fortune. They spent an agonizing 90-day journey traveling the rough terrain to their destination. Like most young men, including his bandit cousin George Washington Loomis, Jr., Thaddeus was forced to admit his failure and after five years of trying to strike it rich he returned home in 1854.

Thaddeus realized it was probably time to settle down to the rural farm life that brought his father to Carlinville. He married Sarah Duckles during the winter of his return.

He soon became restless. He missed the adventures of his time out west and realized that a quiet farming life wouldn't keep him satisfied. In 1857, Thaddeus sold his farm and moved to a new location in Carlinville where he began a new venture of operating a sawmill. The negotiating skills he learned at law school came in handy when he brokered a deal with the Chicago and Alton Railroad, selling them railroad ties and timber. He quickly became known as an astute business man who knew how to turn a profit. Having made a considerable amount of money with the railroad deal, he purchased additional land in Carlinville, which would be known as the Loomis Addition.

You can see how those in town would take notice of Thaddeus and his accomplishments, which is why when the Democratic party was looking for a candidate for county judge in 1861, they called on Thaddeus Loomis. Thaddeus not only won the judge's seat but also won the respect of the citizens with his management of county funds. He even orchestrated paying off nearly $200,000 of existing county debt.

The now seasoned Judge Thaddeus Loomis was up for re-election in 1865. At this time, the county was discussing a new courthouse and opinions on the matter weren't in short supply. Judge Loomis was vocal in his support for a new courthouse and citizens who agreed lent him their vote, which resulted in another victory. Building of the new courthouse began in 1867 and there

THE LOOMIS HOUSE HOTEL

was no question that the honest and intelligent Judge Loomis would be front and center to oversee the construction and finances.

Unfortunately for Judge Loomis, his popularity with the people of Macoupin County would soon take a hit. Soon after building began, the budget on the courthouse exploded to amounts unforeseen by the public. Speculation started as to whether Judge Loomis was simply mismanaging the money or orchestrating a cut for himself. Matters soon became even more complicated. As the construction began to slow down on the Courthouse, people noticed another construction site taking shape on the town square. This building site belonged to Judge Loomis, who was constructing a magnificent hotel. Many people began to fear that Judge Loomis was stealing courthouse funds. It didn't help that architect E.E. Meyers, the same architect responsible for the courthouse, was hired by Judge Loomis to build the

Loomis Hotel, leading to a theory that perhaps Mr. Meyers' architecture bill from the courthouse also went towards the hotel.

It became even more suspicious when County Clerk George Holiday, who was facing his own scandal with the county courthouse, became an investor in the hotel. The theory was that Judge Loomis and Clerk Holiday used tax payer funds and loans for the courthouse to pay for the hotel construction. To add fuel to the fire, the Loomis Hotel held a striking resemblance to the county courthouse. It was undeniable that the same limestone that was paid for by taxpayers for the courthouse looked a lot like the limestone for the Loomis Hotel.

Shortly after the courthouse was finished, the Loomis House Hotel opened in 1870. It contained four floors with more than 50 rooms and a large dining area. It was impressive to say the least -- perhaps too impressive. One angry citizen posted an open letter in several area papers asking Loomis, "Who pays the Courthouse contractors for the building of your house [Loomis House Hotel]?"

Loomis never formally addressed any of the speculation about corruption with the building the Loomis House Hotel or the new courthouse. However, Judge Loomis did admit some of the hotel's limestone was taken from the courthouse project, noting that it was "leftovers" that he had obtained legally. Proof of his legal purchase of the material never seemed to materialize and even if it had, many citizens would've considered it forged, as trust in the Judge had virtually disappeared.

Judge Loomis spent very little time on the bench at the new courthouse, spending most of his time at the hotel. Despite the scandal of the hotel's construction, locals warmed up to the idea of a luxurious hotel in town. The Loomis House Hotel brought in a new wave of business for the downtown Carlinville area. It hosted a variety of people, including entertainers, circus performers, politicians, and traveling salesman. The hotel continued to grow and eventually housed, two stores, a barbershop, a banking office, as well as a saloon and billiards room on the first floor. The hotel saw many events including weddings, dance competitions, and even hunting dinners where men would bring in their game from local hunts and serve a meal at the hotel.

The hotel became known for first-class accommodations, as well as entertainment that became one of Carlinville's worst kept secrets -- the infamous "Loomis Girls." It was hotel manager William Siemens who was known to provide entertainment for those who visited the hotel by offering the company of the "girls" to men who were passing through town. The Loomis ladies of the night became a fixture on the Carlinville square. Back in the late 1800s, many young women had little opportunity for career advancement. If you weren't married, you likely only had a few career options:

school teacher, secretary, or prostitute. Being a lady of the night was not only dangerous due to threats of disease, rape, and domestic violence, but also it was a criminal act that many townspeople detested. In December 1868, the *Alton Telegraph* reported that a prostitute was publicly stoned near White Hall, Illinois, a little over 30 miles from Carlinville in the next county over.

Some people will swear up and down that the "Loomis girls" were a figment of wild imagination, with no physical proof. To that I must answer, can we really believe that a hotel, whether in the late 1800s or current day, is *ever* free of prostitution, one of the oldest professions in history? I don't think so. It seems that those who used the services of the young women did their best to cover up their liaisons but failed to stop the town's dirty little secret from spreading.

Oddly enough, it wasn't the presence of the "Loomis girls" that caused the hotel's downfall; it was the manager William Siemens. Siemens, while small in stature, wielded a lot of power and often became cocky about bending the rules. A few years into operation, Siemens was accused of violating Illinois Liquor laws and the bar was shut down. Judge Loomis, now retired from the bench, had a difficult time paying his own tab and the hotel was put up for sale in May 1875 for $35,000. The next month, the hotel was in foreclosure and in possession of Chestnut and Dubois Banking in Carlinville with reports that $24,814 was left on a mortgage that originally totaled $40,000. However, the hotel didn't stay in the banks hands for long.

Chestnut and Dubois had a very rich Carlinville history. In August 1857, John A. Chestnut, a local attorney, opened the town's first bank. Chestnut eventually left his role as a lawyer to devote his time to the bank full-time. By 1858, the bank was known as Chestnut, Blackburn, and Dubois. A.M Blackburn, son of Gideon Blackburn, founder of the college, resigned that same year and it was announced that a new building would house the bank, where Karla's Jewelry is now located. John Chestnut and Alexander Dubois quickly became a part of Carlinville's high society.

The bank was housed on the first floor of the building with doctor and lawyer offices on the second floor. One of the town's two newspapers, the *Macoupin Spectator*, operated on the top floor. Chestnut and Dubois were local town heroes, as they brought new business and a sense of pride to Carlinville with their successful banking ventures. It made sense that Chestnut and Dubois were appointed as the official bank and agent for the sale of the courthouse bonds during the construction of the new courthouse. The bank was well-respected and trusted to handle the important task of keeping the county's money safe.

THE MACOUPIN COUNTY COURTHOUSE CAN BE SEEN IN THE
BACKGROUND OF THE ST. GEORGE HOTEL
(FORMER LOOMIS HOUSE HOTEL)

The good times didn't last long for Chestnut and Dubois. The courthouse controversy caused outrage in the town and anger was partially focused on the once-respected bank. Those who had business in the building, including the *Macoupin Spectator*, eventually moved out and decided it might be best not to associate with the firm.

While the bank was never formally accused of any wrong-doing, the public perception had already ruined the its reputation. In 1878, the bank was closed, and the building sold.

The hotel was stranded. It initially spent some time in the hands of William Robertson, a wealthy farmer who was strictly against alcohol. Unfortunately, the people of Macoupin County loved their liquor and a ban on the sale of alcohol at the hotel closed the place down. The hotel was soon sold at auction to George Simondson of Decatur, Illinois, and the name was changed to the St. George Hotel in an effort to escape the tarnished Loomis name. In 1909, Theodore C. Loeur opened a pharmacy on the lower level and the building continued to house Carlinville businesses, including a successful bakery.

In the 1950s, the Carlinville Elks club bought the hotel and used it for two decades. In 1975, the Perardi family purchased the old building from the

Loeur's Drug Store on located inside the Loomis House in 1910

Elks and changed the name back to Loomis House. They also opened an attached bar dubbed the St. George Room, which is still in operation. Since that time, numerous business have come and gone out of the Loomis House Hotel but the ghost stories remain consistent.

Stories of the hotel's hauntings go back over 100 years. I must admit, many of these ghost stories rely on urban legend or unverified history but even so, the vast number of haunted happenings leads me to believe that something unusual is happening in the old hotel.

One of the most popular ghosts at the Loomis House Hotel was said to originate when the building was under the operation of the Elks Club. It was known that men who were down on their luck, kicked out the house by their wife, or wanted to sleep off having too much whisky, would occasionally stay at the Elks Club Hotel. One such gentleman was said to be living in the hotel in the 1960s. One night, he was walking down the main staircase when he lost his footing and fell. The man tumbled down the staircase and snapped his neck, dying instantly. The staircase where the alleged fall occurred has been reported as one of the haunted hot spots in the building. Some have described the feeling of being watched, while others have claimed to see a shadowy figure out of the corner of their eye. When they turn to see who is there, the figure vanishes.

American Hauntings' own John Winterbauer, a seasoned paranormal investigator, Haunted Decatur tour guide, and all-around entertaining fellow, (not to mention one of the biggest fans of KISS, Star Wars, and Abraham Lincoln) was one of the last people to investigate the Loomis House before the building was closed to paranormal investigations. John was gracious enough to allow me to use and retell his stories and experiences here.

It's important to note that after the Elks Hotel moved out of the Loomis House, a restaurant moved into the second floor of the hotel. During an investigation that John was on in 2003, he learned it was during the hotel's time as a restaurant that paranormal activity began to peak. Specifically, John was told about a waitress named Gussie, who experienced a frightening event.

Gussie was preparing to open the restaurant for the start of the day. She was alone in the former hotel, or so she thought. As she exited the kitchen she noticed a man standing in the middle of the dining room. Likely a bit annoyed that a customer had snuck into the restaurant before it was time to open, she sighed and began to walk over to the man to ask him to come back later when they started serving. Gussie made it about halfway across the room, when the man vanished right before her eyes. She couldn't believe it! The man had literally disappeared into thin air. Gussie ran out of the restaurant screaming. She never worked alone in the restaurant again.

I experienced an interesting tie-in regarding Gussie's sighting. During the Haunted Carlinville walking tour, I take people up to the Loomis House Hotel to tell a few stories. One evening, I noticed that as we approached the building, one of the men on my tour had become increasingly uncomfortable. Although he appeared to be in his 50's and in no way reserved, he treated the building like a venomous snake. As the man sighed and paced, I asked if everything was all right. He shook his head and proceeding to tell me about his experiences. "I won't get near that building," the man vowed.

He said that he worked at the restaurant in the hotel and one day while completing his everyday tasks, he noticed a man standing in the dining area. He didn't think anything of it until the man disappeared right in front of him. He stood there, astonished about what he just witnessed. It seems that Gussie wasn't the only one who saw the man's apparition.

One of the other locations known for paranormal activity is the St. George Room Bar, which occupies a portion of the original Loomis House Hotel. I'm always extra skeptical when it comes to ghost stories told by those in a bar since clarity might be somewhat skewed. Even so, some patrons recall stories that would have sobered up the drunkest man. John recalled a story he was told by the building's owner regarding a man who was having a drink with some friends at the bar. He looked over and noticed a man standing alone in the room. He had a turn-of-the-century suit on and sported a thick white beard. Obviously, this man stuck out like a sore thumb. The man nudged his friends to point to the odd-looking gentleman but when he turned back to see him, he was gone. Over the years I've also heard stories concerning the bar. Several have reported feeling as though an otherworldly presence was watching them, so much in fact that they end up leaving the bar or stepping outside for some fresh air. It's undeniable that an energy still exists within the bar walls.

Access to the upper floors was still available in the early 2000s, however, the top floors, specifically the third and fourth, were in rough shape. Rooms were water damaged, paint was peeling, and even dead birds were scattered through the building. The old hotel was a far cry from what it used to be, but if you looked hard beyond the dirt and grime,

PHOTOS INSIDE OF THE LOOMIS HOUSE, TAKEN BY TROY TAYLOR IN 2003

you could see the history and grandness of the hotel. John was lucky enough to see this hidden gem up close and personal during a paranormal investigation.

John recalled that he began his investigation on the third-floor near the bridal suite. He was accompanied by a couple of investigators and a sensitive that he trusted named Jenny. John was carrying an EMF meter to see if there was any change in the electro-magnetic field. There was no power in the upper floors of the Loomis Hotel, so any significant changes would be something to note. Suddenly, a cold blast of air hit John and his EMF meter signaled a strong increase. After a few seconds, the temperature returned to normal and the EMF signal dissipated. John tried to recreate the EMF spike, but he couldn't, and to this day cannot explain what happened.

Almost immediately after John's cold encounter, Jenny told John that she had just been to the bridal suite and saw a man in a dark suit with a pocket watch proudly displayed. He was about 6'3, in his mid-forties, and was cradling something like you would cradle a baby. Jenny then made an astounding claim -- she said the man communicated with her and told her, "find me in the armoire." He then stepped through the wall. John was on the other side of that wall and believes the coldness and spike in the EMF was possibly that spirit passing through.

As outstanding as Jenny's claims appeared to be, any doubters during the investigation would soon become believers. John recalls that during the investigation, an antique armoire was indeed discovered on the second floor. Inside was an old photograph of three men standing in front of a dry goods store on the Carlinville square. The men were identified as F.L.J. Breymann, Albert Muller, and William Grotefendt. Jenny took one look at the photograph and immediately identified Mr. Breymann as the man she saw in the bridal suite. Mr. Breymann operated a dry goods and ready-to-wear store next to the Loomis House Hotel. He took over the business in 1919 from Chapino and Giliman, who originated the business in 1872.

While I don't want to discredit Jenny's identification of the apparition she witnessed, I must point out that F.L.J. Breymann was born in 1880, which was after the Loomis House Hotel had closed and changed to the St. George Hotel. Now that doesn't mean that the spirit wasn't Mr. Breymann but it does lead me believe that if it was, it wasn't the history of the Loomis Hotel that brought him there. As far as the apparition's cradling goes, I don't have any legitimate explanation, which leads to even more mystery.

John would return to the Loomis House Hotel again and this time he took Central Illinois on the ride with him. Local WDBR radio and a cameraman from WICS, Channel 20 news, Springfield's local television station, joined John in an attempt to broadcast the paranormal. Jenny, the sensitive from the

EVEN OUTSIDE, MANY ORIGINAL FEATURES OF THE LOOMIS HOUSE HOTEL ARE PRESENT

other investigation, also joined John and was the first to experience something supernatural that night. Jenny said that on the spiral staircase, she met a maid and was able to ask her name. The maid responded with "Isabel."

The legend of Isabel is not new. In fact, she is probably the most talked-about ghost at the Loomis House Hotel. The legend goes that Isabel was not just a young maid, she was also a "Loomis girl" who worked turning tricks to support herself. One night, she was outed as a working girl and, in order to distance themselves away from the scandal, the Loomis House Hotel fired her. Some also say that Isabel was having an affair with a hotel employee and killed herself on the property. Interestingly, Isabel doesn't seem tied down to any particular area of the building. She has been sighted, and her presence felt, throughout the hotel, over several decades.

Old basements tend to give off an unsettling vibe and the basement of the Loomis House Hotel is no different. Since its creation, the hotel basement has housed various businesses, ranging from a barbershop to a bakery. Glass panels in the outside walkway allowed for light to fill the basement and offered a fresh look to an otherwise dark space. Over the years, I've heard stories of a phantom smell of bread baking that lingers around the hotel. I

THE LOOMIS HOUSE HOTEL TODAY

have to say, that is probably one of the most pleasant paranormal interactions that you can hope for! The basement has been vacant of any businesses for the better half of the last century, yet some who pass by the hotel will swear they smell the sweet aroma of freshly baked goods. I even had one woman tell me that she would smell peppermint coming out of the building during her early morning walks. The source of the sweet smells was never explained.

John has investigated the basement several times. He recalls that during one of the paranormal investigations, he placed a recorder near the location that once housed the bakery. The recorder was left for some time as the investigators stepped away. When they returned they heard a very clear EVP saying "stop," giving an ominous warning to those who were near.

On another occasion, he reports that two investigators were in the basement area located under the St. George Room bar, which is used for storage. They noticed a door that had a padlock on it but wasn't latched. As they walked past it, the padlock started to shake. There was no one visibly present shaking the lock but it continued for nearly a minute. Once the shaking stopped, they opened the door to find nothing other than stored bottles.

John recalls that during the time of the rattling padlock, other investigators were on the second floor. One of the men noticed some strange movement. He glanced into a room and noticed something moving back and forth. As he looked closer, he saw a fork that was hung on the wall swaying back and forth. No one had been touching it.

By now, you've likely realized that John has spent numerous hours investigating the Loomis House Hotel and doesn't get startled easily. That would soon change. At the end of an investigation, John was heading up the main staircase and stopped at the landing to take a few more photos. After finishing, he began to pack up his things. Suddenly, he felt he wasn't alone. The sensation of hands caressing his back and his arms washed over him. The embrace eventually dissipated, and John decided it was time to leave.

Employees of the St. George Room bar have also reported haunted happening in the basement. During the Macoupin County Fall Festival, one woman came up to our American Hauntings booth and began to explain that she was a former bartender at the St. George Room. She explained that the bar stored a lot of their alcohol in the basement area, so bartenders were often required to go down there to retrieve it. She reported that, on numerous occasions, she would be collecting alcohol for the bar and would hear footsteps in the basement behind her. She looked back to find herself alone in the dark, deserted basement. She knew that any time she entered the basement there was someone watching her, perhaps making sure she picked the right alcohol for her customers or just making sure their presence was known.

Other spirits said to occupy the hotel include a young bellboy that people have dubbed "Sid Parker." Rumor says that Sid was romantically involved with a maid at the hotel. Stories about why Sid haunts the hotel vary. Some say Sid was fired from his position and died shortly after. He is said to return to the hotel in search of the housemaid he loved. Others have speculated that he was murdered in the hotel and is unaware of his passing, as he continues to search for his lover. His presence has been felt specifically in the maid's quarters and tends to make itself known through empathic means, causing the living person to feel Sid's despair, loneliness, and longing for love.

Of course, one of the most widely rumored spirits in the hotel is that of Judge Thaddeus Loomis himself. After the hotel was handed over to the banking firm of Chestnut and Dubois, Thaddeus' health began to quickly decline. He went to live with his daughter, Mrs. B. L. Dorsey, in Alton, away from the Carlinville scandal. Due to reasons not publicly known, he became paralyzed and deemed an invalid. Thaddeus relied on nurses for all his needs and unfortunately spent the last six years of his life in misery. Thaddeus

Loomis passed away on January 15, 1910, at the age of 85. The only time he would return to Carlinville was for his burial in Carlinville City Cemetery.

Over the years, people have reported seeing a man with a thick gray beard out of the corner of their eye or walking through doorways. This man has also been reported to show up in photographs taken in the hotel, specifically in reflections of glass and mirrors. Due to Judge Loomis' unmistakable signature gray beard, people believe this man is none other than the Loomis house creator himself, finally able to enjoy the hotel he lost.

While some spirits seem to have been identified or at least named, there is still paranormal activity that hasn't been attributed to any certain ghost. Doors slamming shut with no known explanation and the sounds of footsteps when no one is present have been reported in virtually every part of the hotel. It's very possible that the bulk of activity is part of a residual haunting, where energy has been housed in the hotel and events repeat themselves over and over again like an old recording.

In more recent years, the doors of the Loomis House Hotel were opened to psychics, who participated in giving readings to customers, contining to perpetuate the idea that this building is haunted. Unfortunately, when it comes to most psychics and sensitives, though, it's impossible to prove that what they are saying and experiencing is authentic.

The Loomis House Hotel holds numerous stories I can't verify, but even so, I find it hard to ignore the paranormal claims -- simply because of the sheer number that exist. Whether it's an employee in the St. George bar, an old restaurant worker, a customer, or even just a passerby, people are experiencing similar supernatural events.

And they are events that many of them will never forget.

SHOP 'TILL YOU DROP.... DEAD

Next to the notorious Loomis House Hotel, you will find another building made of limestone and much like the Loomis House, the stone seems to be harboring memories of the past. The building was constructed in the late 1860s and in 1875, it became a clothing store founded by William Surman. William's family moved to Carlinville in 1867 and two years later, he attended Blackburn College. His father, Fredrick, was a teacher and merchant and his mother, Fredricka, were German immigrants who originally settled in Indiana before coming to Illinois. As a young man, William become employed as a clerk at a dry goods store, where he became familiar with the business, so familiar, in fact, that he decided to open his own store.

Surman Clothing became a successful fixture in Carlinville and was eventually passed on to William's son, Theodore, in 1934 but that almost wasn't the case. In 1914, Theodore was on a passenger train headed to St. Louis when it struck a freight train that was also traveling southbound near Granite City, Illinois. Theodore was thrown from his seat but survived. A man named John E. Travers of Shipman, Illinois, wasn't as lucky and was consumed by a fire that broke out after the crash.

Theodore's good luck also made its way into the family business, which continued to flourish. Theodore operated the clothing store until his death in 1964. A few years later, the store changed families and was purchased by Louis Ricchiardi, who continued the business. After the Ricchiardis sold the building, it went through many changes, becoming apartments and a variety of different businesses.

In 2017, the owners of Lil' Bits Clothing, Stacy and Dawn, contacted me regarding their newly-opened second-hand store in the old Surman Clothing building. They had many strange tales to tell and I was more than happy to listen. They believed there were several spirits occupying the building, some of which were children. They became aware of the presence of a young girl when one of the owner's two-year-old granddaughter visited the store. The granddaughter would often appear to be speaking to another child, although no other children were present. When she was asked who she was speaking to or playing with, she replied it was a little girl. She described this girl as having blonde hair pulled into a ponytail and wearing a long dress and high shoes. Children tend to have active imaginations, right? Perhaps she was just pretending? The existence of the new "friend" seemed to be confirmed when one day the granddaughter was rolling a ball down the aisle of the store and it rolled back, although there was no one on the receiving end.

THE LIL' BITS STOREFRONT

The little girl appears to have some of her own company in the store. When Dawn was casually walking from one end of the store to another, she noticed a little boy in the middle of the store. As soon as Dawn realized that the store was empty of shoppers, he disappeared. There is also unexplained movement in the store. In the entrance area, you would find racks of clothing for sale. On several occasions, the clothes on the racks would sway back and forth as though someone brushed against them while walking past. The problem was – no one was there. At first, one may assume there was an odd breeze that could have passed through the building or maybe the witness is just imagining things, but after it happens several times and there is no draft present, you begin to accept it was unexplainable.

In addition to the phantom clothing shopper, there is other strange movement in the store. On one of the front walls of the building there were some pictures hanging up for sale. One day, staff in the back of the shop, heard a loud crash and when they investigated, found a picture on the floor. It had knocked over a lamp when it fell. Initially, they rationalized the incident as a case of a picture improperly secured to the wall or as old building that shifted and caused the photo to fall. The strange thing was that other items, not only the photos hanging on the wall, also randomly fell to the ground. Some items had been firmly in place. They tested the wall hanging by jumping up and down and shaking the area, but nothing happened. It appeared someone, or something, was knocking over the items.

Unexplained noises were also a common occurrence at Lil' Bits. The sounds of people chattering in the empty building happened on a regular basis. Even the sounds of items shuffling, or crashing, would be heard when nothing had actually moved. Even more disturbing was a woman's scream that was heard coming from the basement one afternoon. Of course, this alarmed the owners, who immediately opened the basement door only to find the room empty. Anytime strange noises were heard, Stacy and Dawn would do their best to find a reasonable explanation, even checking with the resident of the apartment above them, but would often find that she wasn't home at the time.

The apartments of the building are known to house their own spirits. Ten years prior to the existence of Lil' Bits, Dawn actually lived in the apartment on the second floor. During her residence, she recalled hearing disembodied voices and the sound of boots walking above her on the third floor, which was used for storage. Out of curiosity, Dawn decided to venture up to the third floor and as she glanced around, she saw a figure in the corner. Looking closer, the figure resembled a stocky man who was wearing the clothing of either a railroad worker or miner. The figure faded away.

There was no one living on the third floor – but someone was calling it home.

When you hear haunted tales as grand as the ones from Lil' Bits, there was no option but to conduct a paranormal investigation. In the Summer of 2017, I was joined by American Hauntings' guides and authors, Len Adams and Luke Naliborski, to see if we would be lucky enough to have an experience similar to Stacy and Dawn.

Before beginning, we explored the building. We had full access to the first floor and the basement but were not allowed to investigate the second or third floor. The store was full of merchandise, which meant we would need to get creative and make do with the small amount of free space we had. In addition to using EMF meters, we also had cameras and Len's classic bell system, which included placing bells on a string surrounding the area in which the spirit of the young boy was seen. The hope was that we would hear the bells ring if there was any movement in that area.

We also wanted to see if we could capture the spirit of the young girl and we placed a ball on the floor to see if we could replicate the ball rolling on its own. A camera was setup to monitor the area, with the ball's position marked to confirm any movement.

As with any paranormal investigation, there was a lot of sitting, waiting, and listening. At the beginning of the investigation, I noticed voices coming from the back of the building. Upon checking out the area it seemed the back of the building might be susceptible to sounds from the bar next door. It's possible that some of the voices and crashing noises could be coming from the neighboring building.

The most interesting part of the investigation was the basement, which is difficult to access. In fact, the only way down to the basement is by ladder and a bit of a jump. I was hesitant to go into the dirty, treacherous basement but after hearing movement coming from that area, I had no choice. I mustered up the courage to descend the rickety ladder and found myself in a dirt- and sand-floored basement. There were no signs of any critters causing the noises but there was something that sparked my interest. It looked as though there was an opening that had been boarded up on the side of the basement wall. The first thought that popped into my mind was, "Could this be an access for the rumored tunnels that ran under Carlinville?"

I was reminded of the woman's scream that had been heard coming from basement and I couldn't help but wonder if the basement of this building was connected to the Loomis House Hotel through the tunnels, which some believe were used by prostitutes in the late 1800s and early 1900s. At this point, I could only speculate where the opening in the basement once led.

The rest of our night was uneventful. The bells on the string didn't ring and the ball on the floor didn't move. We didn't capture any EVPs and we didn't have much to report back to Stacy and Dawn. However, just because we didn't have evidence doesn't mean there isn't something paranormal happening in the building.

Stacy and Dawn weren't present for the investigation and I think it might have yielded some results if they had, specifically from the spirits of the children, who may have felt a familiarity with them.

Unfortunately, Lil' Bits clothing is no longer in the building and it currently sits empty. I'm hoping the next business will keep us in mind if the spectral sightings or blood-curdling screams start again. Until then, the mystery of the building remains.

TRAGEDY ON THE SQUARE
A FAMILY NIGHTMARE IN CARLINVILLE

One of the most frequent questions I've been asked regarding hauntings is "why do they always involve people and events from so long ago? Aren't there any new ghosts?" Instead of hearing reports of ghostly big band music playing from a haunted house, why don't we hear about a supernatural rendition of "Baby Got Back?"

I understand why people ask this question. Most of the ghost stories we hear involve someone from 100 years ago and from a time that we only know through history books. The truth is, though, there are numerous newly haunted places but many times the events that led to the haunting are too fresh for those living to discuss out in the open. One of the most tragic tales in Carlinville happened on the square within the last 50 years and during the lifetime of many area residents. If you didn't live through it or you don't ask about it directly, you probably haven't heard the story.

On December 18, 1968, the Kline family gathered at the DCFS office located on the 2nd floor of Burke pharmacy on the town square. They had hoped for a joyous Christmas celebration as a family, but it would soon turn into pure horror.

The Kline family had been unstable for a very long time. Prior to the scheduled meeting at the DCFS office in Carlinville, the family lived in Brussels, Illinois, located in Calhoun County. The family consisted of Sherman and Lorraine Kline and their 10 children. Lorraine would often leave the home, either to obtain employment in Missouri or more often to escape Sherman, who had a history of violent outbursts. Eventually, she would find her way back to the trailer with her family and things would remain peaceful -- at least for a while.

They were a hard luck family. Even with Sherman working across the river in St. Louis as a plumber and Lorraine working odd jobs, taking care of the seven children still at home was nearly impossible. Those in the community took notice of the fact that the children didn't seem to have clean clothes for school and many worried they were not getting enough to eat. It was widely known that the Kline children were largely responsible for themselves, having very little supervision at home.

Calhoun County Sheriff Bernard Killen took notice of the Kline family and decided it was time to involve Children and Family Services in Carlinville, since their office was also responsible for Calhoun County. The goal was the keep the family together and offer some assistance to the Klines. One of the family service employees, which they called a homemaker, was sent to assist and teach the family how to provide a better home life. She would help them prepare food, clean up the house, and ready the children for school. For the few weeks the homemaker visited the Klines, life seemed to improve but unfortunately the bliss did not last. Sherman was less than thrilled that an outsider was taking care of his family and made it clear that the homemaker was no longer welcome.

A young 24-year-old social worker named Frank Wildgrube was then appointed to the family. Frank was a devout Catholic who had a passion for family reconciliation and believed redemption was possible for everyone, even the erratic Sherman Kline. As Frank approached the Kline trailer for a visit, Sherman stood at the door and pulled out an automatic pistol. Before Frank had realized it, Sherman had put a clip into the gun and pulled the trigger. Nothing happened. Within what appeared to be a split second, Sherman reloaded the bullet and fired again near Frank's feet. With Frank in complete shock, Sherman took a wild swing at him but luckily, Frank was able to leave the property with his life and foot intact.

SHERMAN KLINE

Assault charges were filed against Sherman Kline for the assault on Frank Wildgrube. Sheriff Killen was sent to find Sherman and bring him into custody. The sheriff heard that Sherman was at his daughter Linda's school, so the police rushed over. Prior to the sheriff arriving, Sherman had already made a call to the Family Services Office in Carlinville from the Superintendent's desk. The Carlinville office pleaded with Sherman to turn himself in, but Sherman refused. He was adamant that nobody could help him. A few minutes into the phone call, Sheriff Killen arrived at the school and Sherman abruptly hung up the phone. As the sheriff entered the superintendent's office, Sherman pulled out a .25 caliber pistol and fired, barely missing the sheriff. Sherman was ordered to put down the gun but instead, he took his daughter hostage, holding a gun to her head and threatening to shoot her if the sheriff came near him. Realizing Sherman wasn't afraid of pulling the trigger, the sheriff backed away and Sherman fled from the school. He was now a fugitive.

Sherman escaped across the river on his boat and additional warrants were issued for his arrest. The Kline children were then taken from their home in Brussels and placed into several foster homes in the area. About a month later, the police learned Sherman was arranging to meet his wife in St. Louis at a gas station. They planned to arrive before Sherman did and stake out the area, but they arrived too late. Sherman was already at the station and in a car with his wife and her friend when the police arrived. Sherman spotted the police and quickly grabbed his wife, putting a pistol to her head. Sherman then exited the car with his terrified wife, boasting that he would shoot her if the police came any closer. One of the St. Louis officers noticed that Sherman was momentarily distracted by another officer and decided to make a move. He lunged at Sherman and was able to free Lorraine and knock the pistol out of his hand. Finally, Sherman was taken into custody.

Sherman became an inmate at the St. Louis County Jail. Soon after arriving, he tried to overdose on sleeping pills but survived. His act of self-harm further intrigued the officers, who were curious as to what made this violent man tick. During interviews at the jail, Sherman reported he had "cracks in his head." He said every night he would have severe migraines that would lead to memory loss. Sherman would also become distracted easily and appear to drift off in thought, even when engaging in direct conversation. He was eventually transported to a psychiatric hospital in St. Louis. Psychiatrist Dr. Joseph S. Shuman diagnosed Sherman with "psychoneurosis with hysterical conversion reaction, and psychopathic personality disorder of the antisocial type." After three weeks in the psychiatric hospital, bail was arranged for Sherman by his employer for the charges in Illinois and Missouri. After posting bail, Sherman began living in a trailer in St. Louis and returned to work.

Shockingly, Sherman still had visitation rights to his children. A meeting was arranged in October at the Carlinville Family Services offices and everything seemed normal -- or as normal as possible regarding the situation. At first, it seemed that Sherman was going to make amends for his actions, even pleading guilty to the charges, but it was all for show. Sherman's parole officer reported that Sherman refused to accept that he was the reason for the breakup of his family. He blamed it on his wife, who he said drank too much, and, of course, on Carlinville social worker Frank Wildgrube.

Over the next couple of months, Sherman faced sentencing in Missouri and realized he would likely go to prison. He was in debt for the bail money his employer spent and for numerous other expenses that he couldn't afford. He lost custody of his children and found out his wife was seeing another man. This time, she likely wouldn't return home. Sherman was going to lose everything, and he was getting increasingly desperate.

Sherman and Lorraine were both scheduled to visit their children on December 18 at the Carlinville family services office. Sherman drove his brother Vernon's car from O'Fallon, Missouri, and offered to pick up his wife and two of his children -- Linda, who at age 15 had recently married, and 14-year-old Michael. Michael had recently run away from his foster home. Unbeknownst to family services, he had rejoined his parents.

At around 2:50 p.m., Sherman arrived in Carlinville with his family. They joined five other Kline children, who were brought in by social workers, including Frank Wildgrube, who, despite being shot at by Sherman, was still working with the family.

The children gathered around a Christmas tree in the office, anxiously waiting to open presents. Before the festivities could begin, Frank pulled Sherman aside after noticing Michael was there. Linda was old enough to make her own decisions, but Michael was technically a runaway and Sherman had no right to transport or house his son. Sherman was furious and the two exchanged words in the hallway.

Suddenly, gun shots echoed throughout the building. Sherman had pulled out two pistols and shot Frank directly in the head. Lorraine ran out into the hallway and Sherman fired again, killing his wife. Sherman then ran into the office where the Christmas tree was. He began shooting and didn't stop until nothing was moving.

He then started opening other office doors in the building and found the desks of Mrs. Edward Albracht Jr., a social worker, and soon to be married Ann Harriette Keppler, a secretary. Miss Keppler quickly stood up in front of another secretary, Mary Lou Stolps, who was facing Sherman. Sherman fired, killing Mrs. Albracht and Ann Keppler.

The silence that followed the thunderous sounds of the gunshots was broken by a ringing telephone. The sound seemed to snap Sherman out of whatever evil daze he was in and he quickly ran down the stairs, even bumping into the State's Attorney on the street. Sherman quickly piled into the car and made his way back to O'Fallon, Missouri, to his brother Vernon's home. Sherman confessed the murderers to his brother and claimed he was going to kill himself. Before the conversation could go any further, police

THE LOCATION OF THE KLINE MURDERS, WHICH OCCURRED ON THE TOP FLOOR

sirens were heard in the distance and Sherman took off into the woods behind his brother's home. One more gunshot was heard. Sherman had shot himself in the head.

At the family services office in Carlinville, office administrator Ray Unterbrink, who had just parked his car after dropping off some of the Kline children, noticed Sherman running out of the building. Anxious to see what the commotion was about, he walked up the stairs to find devastation and horror.

Blood was splattered on the walls and covered the Christmas decorations and toys. He found a half-eaten apple and lollipop documenting how quickly the shooting spree occurred. Additional personnel and police officers arrived at the office to find more injuries and several fatalities. Three of the Kline children took cover under office desks, which likely saved them. The four other children weren't so lucky. Two of the children were in serious condition and the other two were in critical condition. Eight-year-old Diane Kline was shot in the head and died two days later from her injuries. Michael Kline, who had been the subject of the argument between Sherman and Frank died from his injuries in February 1969.

The day ended with six dead – Sherman's wife, two of his children, two case workers, and a secretary.

Immediately following the discovery of the bodies, area schools went on lockdown, worried that the madman may be out looking for more victims. It wasn't until later that evening that his death was reported. Following the tragedy, more information would be revealed about the violent father. An article in the *Alton Evening Telegraph* featured an interview with Lorraine's sister, Gloria, who recalled that, days prior to the shooting, Sherman had told her, "This is the last time you'll see me alive" and while pointing to a photo of the Kline children he said, "See those kids, they're going to be dead." Sherman then took a handful of sleeping pills and continued to ramble about his plans for destruction. That same day Gloria recalled a happier Sherman who laughed and enjoyed reminiscing about years past. There was no doubting that Sherman was his own version of Dr. Jekyll and Mr. Hyde.

As far as Lorraine's family was concerned it was the sleeping pills and the fear of losing his family that caused Sherman to commit such horrendous acts.

In the end, it appears Sherman did get his family back. Lorraine's family buried Sherman with the wife and two children he brutally murdered.

The tragedy brought unwanted national attention to the quiet town of Carlinville. The townspeople were quick to put this gory past behind them and regain some peace on the square. The children and family services office moved out of the building and the Kline murders became an unspoken secret -- but secrets always have a way of revealing themselves.

During the *Haunted Carlinville Tour*, I tell the story of the Kline murders. More often than not, I have someone pull me to the side and tell me their memories from that day. Some were in school and remember being petrified that a scary monster was coming to get them. Some were friends with the Kline children and remember the tragedy of losing one of their friends. Some even knew one of the employees of the family services office or worked on the square during that time. The sense of panic and loss is present in each of their stories, however, there was one story that had a bit of a twist.

One night after the Kline story was completed, a man pulled me aside and began to tell me his story. He was a bit nervous but spoke with conviction. It was the early 1970s, he said, and he was an out of town student at Blackburn College. Like most college students he was looking for a way to make a few extra dollars and so when he heard about a nighttime janitorial job at the pharmacy on the square he was happy to take it. His job seemed rather straight forward. He would tidy up the building, sweep floors, dust, and basically anything else that needed to be completed. It didn't take long for him to notice the upstairs was eerily different than the downstairs. One of the first odd things he noticed were the hurried upstairs renovations that were not quite complete and a strange reddish hue that appeared on the wall. He would scrub the walls and come back to find that the stain had reappeared. It was frustrating and perplexing to the young college student.

He also couldn't shake the feeling that he was being watched while cleaning the upstairs. Shadows would seem to peek out from behind corners and a sense of dread and unease followed him throughout the upstairs halls. The unsettling feeling became too much to ignore when one night he was cleaning and felt a tug on his shirt tail. It was the tug of a child wanting his attention.

There was, of course, no one there.

The man was reluctant to tell his employer of what had occurred, fearing they would fire him or think he is crazy, but he couldn't go on like this any longer. He worked up the courage and told his boss about what he experienced. His boss sighed and told him the story of Sherman Kline and the six deaths that occurred that dreaded afternoon in 1968.

The Burke's pharmacy building has gone through many changes over the years but still holds the history and energy of Sherman Kline's actions. After learning about the paranormal activity experienced in the building, I decided to make a very awkward visit to the current pharmacy that occupied the building. I spoke to one of the employees and explained my affiliation with American Hauntings. In the most normal way possible, I asked that they contact me if there was anything unusual that happened in the building.

The response I received was, "Oh, you mean the ghost children upstairs?" I nodded, and they took my card.

The haunting of the pharmacy on the square shows us that not all spirits are unfamiliar legends and not all hauntings are long ago tales.

DINNER AND SPIRITS

Like every small town, Carlinville has its own legends that tread the fine line between fact and fiction. Perhaps one of the most widely-known legends is that of a man named Angus Bailey. The story goes that he was a loner who rode into town on a cold winter night in 1893. He was looking for something to eat and a stiff drink to warm him up when he wandered into a saloon on the North Side of the Carlinville Square.

Angus took off his hat and walked up to the bar. As he was getting ready to enjoy his drink and meal, he began to hear the rumblings of a few men in

EARLY PHOTO OF LOCALS ENJOYING THE CARLINVILLE SQUARE

the bar, specifically a troublemaker known as Old Man Meriwether. The other men began to call Angus a cattle rustler, which were ugly fighting words in the 1890s. Angus tried to ignore them, but they roughed him up and shoved him out of his chair. A fight ensued, which left poor Angus one man against many.

The brawl continued outside the bar with fists flying in the cold winter air. Even though Angus was a strong man, he was no match against the drunk and angry Carlinville men. One of the men fetched a rope and they proceeded to tie it around Angus's neck. They continued to beat Angus as they drug him by the neck to the back of the saloon, where they finally ended his suffering with a violent hanging.

After the men completed the murder of this poor loner, they took his body outside of town and buried it in an unmarked grave.

Since that time, Angus Bailey has become a legend, rumored to haunt the location of his hanging. In fact, if you fast forward 100 years you would find a restaurant that bore his name – Angus Bailey's. The restaurant boasted about the legend of the murdered man, even including the story on their menu.

Those who worked at or visited the restaurant, lived in the apartments above the building, or even on that side of the square, often reported hearing phantom footsteps in the building and on the nearby street, mainly in the snowy winter months. Are they mistaking the sound of the winter wind or the creaking of the old building? Or are they hearing the footsteps of the unlucky traveler who came to the wrong town?

Legends can be tricky and often stray from the truth. As far as Angus Bailey himself goes, there appears to be no historical evidence of his existence, let alone his murder. I've also been told by some locals that the legend really took off when the restaurant came into existence and was perhaps fabricated, or at the very least exaggerated, to create a buzz.

I can't prove that Angus Bailey existed but even if the origin of the haunting on the North Side of the Square isn't factual, it is undeniable that many still believe the local establishment hangs on to some remnant of the past, making itself known on long winter nights.

Angus Baileys restaurant has since closed their doors but in its place is another notable Carlinville attraction with over 110 years of history -- Taylor's Mexican Chili Parlor. Authentic Mexican chili in a small Illinois town may seem a bit unusual but that's exactly why it works so well. The idea for this unconventional parlor started with Charles O. Taylor.

At the 1904 World's Fair in St. Louis, Charles discovered his love for south of the border cuisine at the Mexico exhibition. The budding entrepreneur had an idea and started to sell tamales to the saloons around the Carlinville square, wheeling them around in a small cart. Thankfully, when people drink they tend to get hungry and Mexican food became all the rage in Carlinville.

Charles realized that if he wanted to expand his business he would need more recipes. The misfortune of a recently arrested Mexican gentleman turned into Charles's solution. Charles made a deal with the jailed man and paid his $3 bail in exchange for the recipe to Mexican chili. The rest is history.

Taylor's Mexican Chili Parlor has been a staple in Carlinville ever since, as had been the personality of Charles Taylor himself. You see, Charles had a peculiar disposition. The best way I can explain it is to refer to an example in the show *Seinfeld*. Remember the soup Nazi? Well, Charles was the chili Nazi. He had specific rules that patrons were to follow or "No chili for you!"

For example:

1. Have your money ready! No fumbling through your purse or wallet for cash. You simply placed your money on the counter and kept moving.
2. No chit chat, no flirting, no business meetings, and no lollygagging! This was a place to eat your chili, not socialize.
3. No rowdy children! While Charles was a family man, the chili parlor was serious business, not to be disrupted by unruly kids.

4. Never ask for ketchup or coffee! The chili was perfect just as it was made. Although vinegar was allowed.

Even with his quirks, everyone loved Taylor's. The parlor began canning its chili as the years went by and introduced additional items including their ever-popular butterbean soup. There was also a gentle side to Charles who was reported to help his fellow citizens during the Great Depression by giving them soup and packaging it in quart containers, so they could feed their families. All jokes aside, he was a beloved character in Carlinville. His chili even reached presidential status in 1976 when a can of it was given to President Gerald Ford when he stopped in Carlinville.

IF YOU CAN'T MAKE IT TO THE RESTAURANT, YOU CAN FIND CANNED TAYLOR'S CHILI IN SEVERAL MACOUPIN COUNTY GROCERY STORES

The Taylor family has since sold the business, but the popularity and recipe are still the same. The chili joint has been featured on The Travel Channel's *Diners, Drive-ins, and Dives* and shipments of the chili have been sent as far away as Japan. Once you have the Mexican chili, you won't be able to forget it!

While there is only one chili parlor in town, Carlinville has its fair share of taverns and has since the first settlers came into town. One of the first six buildings in Carlinville was a saloon, proving early on that Carlinville was the place to stop for a nice drink.

Macoupin County's first "official" tavern -- meaning they paid taxes on the establishment -- was opened in 1830 by owners William S. Holton and Tristram P. Hoxey. The tavern was actually inside the house of Mr. Holton but even so, it offered a large variety of services.

For 25-cents, you could get one of the following: breakfast, lunch, supper, a half pint of rum, wine, or French brandy, or could stable your horse for the night. On a budget? For about 12-cents, you could feed your horse, get a half pint of whisky, or a quart of cider or beer. Looking for an even better bargain? For about 6-cents, you could stay the night. Oddly enough, it was more expensive for your horse to stay the night than it was for you.

It's hard to say how many bars have operated in Carlinville but one that maintains a solid connection to the town's eerie past is Hollywood and Vine on Carlinville's Main Street. The bar plays host to not only devoted regular patrons but also several spirits.

In 2015, the first *Haunted Carlinville tour* took place. Our group of nearly 50 people was strolling down Main Street when we passed the bar. The owner, Debbie, stopped the caboose of the group and asked why all these people were walking around Carlinville. They explained that we were on a haunted history tour and Debbie remarked that we should stop by after the tour for a little chat. We're glad we did.

Debbie explained that she had purchased the bar from her uncle and aunt and has since experienced numerous strange occurrences inside the building. One of the most memorable and personal experiences occurred while Debbie was tending bar. A customer pointed behind her and asked, "Who's that man?" Debbie turned around to find nobody there. At first, she assumed the customer was joking around with her but then he described the man he saw. It was an older gentleman, he said, with a very distinctive hat and overcoat. As the customer continued to describe the man he'd seen, Debbie slowly realized that he was describing her deceased uncle. Not only had Debbie been close to her uncle but as the former owner, he was passionate about the bar. Debbie believes that he stops by once in a while to see how things are going.

It isn't just Debbie's uncle who visits Hollywood and Vine. The identities of other ghostly visitors are more elusive, but their presence is still very much apparent. One of the most haunted areas of the bar is the ladies restroom. Late one evening, Debbie was getting ready to leave but noticed the bathroom door closed. It appeared as though someone was in there, so Debbie waited. She waited, and waited, and waited, until she became concerned. She walked up to the door and knocked. No answer. She then asked out loud if anyone was in there. No answer. After growing increasingly worried about the condition of whoever was inside, she opened the door only to find the bathroom completely empty.

During our *Haunted Carlinville* tours, we stop at Hollywood and Vine for a small break and an adult beverage. One evening, two women decided to take a bathroom trip and went into the ladies restroom. I was standing nearby, chatting with other guests, when the women came out of the restroom a few minutes later. They seemed a bit upset. They asked if anyone else had been in the restroom with them. I knew nobody went in after them and assured them they were alone. They looked at each other with a confused expression and swore up and down they heard footsteps in the bathroom, as well as footsteps coming from above them. Oddly, there is no second story to the bar. There couldn't have been anyone above them – and there had been no one else in the restroom. We were unable to explain what they heard.

Not only are phantom footsteps heard in the bar and restroom, but also in the room in back. In this area, people have heard disembodied female voices. Debbie explained that some of her regulars, specifically women, have heard chatting in this area when nobody else was present. Not only do they hear muffled voices, but some have even heard their name whispered.

One of the most interesting things about the back room is that it shows the building's true age. You can still see the once gorgeous tin ceiling, which was a popular addition in the mid- to late-1800s. Also unique to this area is a door that is hidden under a rug on the floor. I've been told this door leads to a dirty and grimy cellar area. Was this cellar once connected to the tunnels that are believed to have been under Carlinville? We can't say for sure what purpose the cellar once served, but it does lead to a theory regarding an original use for the building.

One of the stories surrounding this back area is that it was once part of a brothel. The working girls would conduct their business in this area and hide in the cellar in the event of a police raid. They also supposedly used it to move from one location to another through the now-elusive tunnel system. There is no historical evidence to prove this story, but it remains a popular explanation for the otherworldly female presence.

On several occasions during our tour stops to this area, women have taken time to sit in this back room and some have reported hearing movement when all was still, as well as hearing that ghostly female chatter. One occasion that I recall concerned a young lady who spent some time in this area and became overwhelmed with emotion. With tears in her eyes she expressed an overwhelming sense of sadness and loneliness that she couldn't shake until she left the bar.

Hollywood and Vine is a prime example of how sometimes we don't know the exact story of the spirits who linger but we can feel their emotion and make a connection nonetheless.

4. HERE WE ARE NOW, ENTERTAIN US
MEDIA AND THEATER IN CARLINVILLE

In the days when you couldn't tweet your every thought, watch 24-hour news, or even listen to the radio, people relied on their local newspapers for information and entertainment. The weeklong wait for the local gossip in the Carlinville newspaper might have been enough to send people these days into a panic, but that was the norm in the 1850s.

HAVE YOU HEARD THE NEWS?

The *Macoupin Statesman* is said to be the first newspaper in Carlinville. It was founded in 1852 and edited by Jefferson L. Dugger, who used the paper to advocate his Whig party beliefs. Unlike today, where the media likes to state its "fairness," whether true or not, media of the 1800s didn't shy away from their obvious bias. When the newspaper changed owners and names in 1855 to the *Macoupin County Spectator*, it also changed its political leanings. The new editor, George Holliday, was a Democrat and, therefore, so was the paper. Holliday was not only the head of the newspaper, but he was also the county clerk. As Holliday's popularity as clerk began to decline due to distrust over county spending, so did his presence at the newspaper.

In 1868, the newspaper underwent another transformation to the *Macoupin Times*, only to become the *Macoupin Enquirer* a few years later. The newspaper continued in operation, fighting the rival *Free Democrat* newspaper until eventually the town could no longer support two fully operational newspapers. The two finally merged into the *Macoupin County Enquirer Democrat (MCED)* in 2003. Before the MCED settled in its current location on Main Street, the newspaper offices were on the south side of the town square. The paper has been owned by the Schitt family for more than 70 years, spanning three generations.

A newspaper with over 165 years of history is bound to have some interesting history but this newspaper also has a dose of ghosts. I learned about the haunted history of the newspaper during my employment at the MCED in 2014. It didn't take long for me to hear the stories of both current and past employees who believed the building to be haunted.

Many people who have worked at the newspaper have experienced unexplained footsteps, heard disembodied voices, witnessed odd shadows, and even felt the touch of an unseen presence. The stories are endless and have been ongoing for decades. One woman who worked upstairs at the newspaper recalled feeling her hand stroked on at least one occasion as well as the sensation of someone playing with her hair. She was in the office alone at the time – or at least she was the only living person. It seems that at least one spirit in the building prefers ladies with curly blonde hair as they are the ones who seem to be touched the most. Luckily for me, I'm a straight-haired brunette.

The manager of the newspaper had her own set of stories. While working late one night she walked downstairs and passed the printing area and noticed a bathroom door open. She didn't think anything of it and began shutting off the downstairs lights. Upon reentering the printing area and preparing to leave, she saw the bathroom door close by itself. She knew she was the last in the building and immediately suspected someone had snuck inside when she wasn't looking. She called out to the person in the bathroom, but nobody answered. Unsettled by the lack of response and suspicion that she wasn't alone, she quickly went outside and locked the newspaper doors. She called her husband, who agreed to come over and check out the building. He entered the building, seeking the unwanted visitor. As he approached the bathroom door, anxious and ready to fight if needed, he opened the door to find nobody was there.

On another night, a manager was working late upstairs. She heard very distinct footsteps climbing the staircase. She yelled out to see who was coming up the steps, thinking it might be one of the reporters, but there was no answer. The footsteps continued and grew louder until they reached the door to the office, where they abruptly stopped all together. After gathering the courage to check and who may be on the other side of the door, she opened it and she found herself alone. She had no logical explanation for what she heard.

Electronics have also been known to go a bit crazy from time to time in the building, including a small clock radio in the billing office. This was witnessed by a receptionist, who decided to come in on a Saturday. She figured that being alone on a quiet weekend morning would allow her to catch up on some unfinished work. She was wrong. The clock radio turned on, blared some music, and then turned off. At first, she assumed the radio must be on a timer. However, it turned on and off again and that's when she realized the clock wasn't on a timer and the door to the billing office was locked with no way for any person, or at least any living person, to turn it on. She quickly packed up her things and decided that she wouldn't work another Saturday by herself again.

During my time at the newspaper, it was not uncommon for me to work at the office at night or be alone in the building. One evening, I was waiting for an event at Blackburn College and heard what sounded like high-heeled shoes coming down the stairs. Knowing that I was the only one in the building, and certainly unaware of any magical self-walking high heels, I went to investigate. I followed the sound out of the room and around the corner towards the stairs. As soon as I peered over to the steps, the sound stopped. I never found the owner of the heels and eventually became accustomed to the odd noises. It was also common to see odd shadows out of the corner of my eye and even witnessed what appeared to be invisible hands flipping through newspapers that were placed in a box.

After hearing the stories and experiencing the unexplained myself, I thought I could take advantage of the Halloween season, and the need to fill some newspaper space, by indulging my own curiosity about the paranormal. I approached the owner and editor of the newspaper with the idea of conducting a paranormal investigation of the building and reporting it in the paper. To my surprise, she agreed.

I had always been fascinated with the paranormal and even lived in a rather haunted house as a child, but my knowledge of ghost hunting ended with corny television shows. I had no idea how to find a paranormal investigator, much less a reputable one, so I did what any person does when they need to find an answer -- I Googled it.

After a quick search of "Central Illinois paranormal investigator" I stumbled upon a man named Troy Taylor. He had written quite a few books about the paranormal and as far as I could tell, didn't scream "serial killer," so I figured I would reach out to him. After some email exchanges, we settled on a date on which he would investigate the newspaper.

It was Columbus Day weekend in 2014 when Troy Taylor and his company manager, Lisa Taylor-Horton, arrived at the paper. I was present with a couple other employees and a few friends of mine who were skeptics. The equipment used for the investigation included a REM pod (a device that would emit a high-pitched squeal when it detected movement), meters to detect EMF fluctuations and temperature, an Ovilus (believed to interpret the surrounding energy and vocalize it into words), and a voice recorder to detect EVPs (electronic voice phenomenon), which are theorized to be the voices of spirits that aren't detectable by the human ear.

THE MACOUPIN COUNTY ENQUIRER-DEMOCRAT NEWSPAPER IN 2018

We set up the REM pod in the billing area of the newspaper and then headed to the distribution room. Two meters both indicated unstable electrical fields in the building but, considering the buildings age and condition, I assumed the poor wiring may have been the cause. However, it didn't take long for us to have our first unexplained experience.

We asked out loud if there was a spirit present and to show itself by making a banging noise. Within a couple seconds we heard a very distinctive bang. At first, I assumed someone was joking around, but everyone swore it wasn't them. The Ovilus also yielding some interesting results. Some of the first words reported were "property," "holiday," "story," and "main". All the words seemed to correlate to the newspaper. The newspaper is on "main" street, the newspaper's main purpose is to tell a "story," and it was a "holiday" weekend. Also, George Holliday was one of the men who owned the newspaper. It seemed far too familiar to be completely circumstantial, but who knows?

We made our way up to the second floor and took a seat in the art department area. As everyone was getting settled, I noticed I was the only one standing since there were no chairs left. I sarcastically asked, "Where am I supposed to sit?" On cue, the Ovilus replied, "Down." Of course, I quickly ran over to a chair my friend was sitting on and made her share. The Ovilus also repeated three words that gave me pause: "Saturn," "tire," and "disaster." At the time, my car was a Saturn and unknown to anyone else that day, I had received my first and only flat tire on my way to the investigation that night. I can't explain why those words would have come through, but they seemed very specific to me. Having received such a personal response, I asked what the spirit thought of a recent story I had written regarding the apple season. The reply was "waste." Like me, the spirit doesn't seem to be a fan of fluff stories.

In a back office, the Ovilus began to speak again, one of the words being "dime." An employee then asked out loud if the spirit was referring to the dime she found earlier that day in the office. At that moment, the electrical field in the room drastically increased and then dissipated. The employee remembered the incident of the dime because she thought it was odd that she would find a random dime on the floor on a Sunday when the office had been closed for the weekend.

We ended our investigation downstairs in the reception area. The Ovilus spoke the word "awards" and "quill." After hearing this, the manager of the newspaper began to seem very anxious. She explained that prior to Troy and Lisa arriving she wanted to straighten up the area and she rearranged some of the awards on the wall, specifically an award with a quill pen on it. The next day the manger made sure to put this award with the quill pen back in the position it was prior to her moving it.

Throughout the investigation Lisa conducted EVP sessions. One of the most interesting captures occurred when we asked, "are you [the spirit] happy with the upcoming election?" At the time we didn't hear a response but upon review of the recording, we heard a very audible "no."

Personally, I was impressed with the activity we captured and witnessed that night. Even those who were skeptics admitted there were things they couldn't explain. After publishing a story about the investigation, one of the former owners stopped by for a visit. He stated that he often felt as though someone was watching him, especially on long stressful nights, almost as though someone, or something, was providing a helpful and supportive presence.

One of the theories about the identity of this spirit is that it may be W.L. Schmitt, a man who spent the majority of his life devoted to the newspaper. He was a passionate man who didn't shy away from the controversial stories or expressing his political opinion. On more than one occasion, he addressed Carlinville citizens personally in the newspaper, calling them out as to why he had an issue with them or why he disagreed with their views. Even so, he was known to be a loving man who cared about the community, his employees, and his family. If there is a spirit present at the newspaper, I think it makes sense that it may be Mr. Schmitt, who, after all these years, is still devoted to the profession he loved so much.

I also think it's possible that the newspaper harbors residual hauntings -- repeating noises, actions, and events of years past. Maybe that would explain some of the footsteps that are heard when nobody is present?

I no longer work at the newspaper, but I will always be thankful for the opportunities that experience gave me. If it wasn't for the newspaper I wouldn't be part of American Hauntings and I wouldn't be writing this book. After the investigation concluded, Troy and Lisa expressed some interest in forming an American Hauntings tour in Carlinville. Luckily, they invited me to create and lead the tour, which is still in operation today. I owe it all to the haunted Macoupin County Enquirer newspaper.

A PHOTO OF W. L. SCHMITT WAS PROUDLY DISPLAYED DURING OUR INVESTIGATION

A HOLLYWOOD MARVEL

In 1882, the first official theater in town, the Carlinville Opera House, opened its doors. The city purchased the Methodist church that was located at the southwest corner of South Broad and First South streets for their new venture. The opera house was complete with an auditorium and stage that brought shows like "Uncle Tom's Cabin" to Carlinville. In the early 1900s, the opera house started showing flickers, an early type of movie that flicked through a series of pictures. It was the precursor to silent films. Ever wonder why we call a movie a "flick?" Well it all started with flickers.

Carlinville would enter a new era of entertainment on August 26, 1920, when Frank and Freida Paul opened the Marvel playhouse. It cost over $40,000 to build (the equivalent of over half a million dollars in today's cash), but for that price, the Pauls acquired what became known as one of the most beautiful theaters in Central Illinois. The Marvel not only brought plays and movies to the area but also acrobats, comedians, and even animal shows. It was the glamorous Freida Paul who took it upon herself to ensure that the area experienced a bit of Hollywood glamour when they walked into the Marvel.

Freida was born March 25, 1893, to Jacob and Mary Stadler Ring in Morrisonville, Illinois. She was the youngest of 10 children but still managed to stand out with her vivacious personality. Music quickly became her passion. She was an accomplished pianist by age five. When she was 20, her life took a tragic turn when her fiancé was killed by a train after dropping her off after a date. In an effort to escape the heartache, Frieda made her way to sunny Los Angeles to visit relatives. In 1914, she began playing the piano for silent films in L.A. and quickly became adept at keeping the audience entertained with her musical skills. She spent a few months in the big city but then returned home to Illinois.

Shortly after returning home, she began dating Frank Paul, who operated a grocery and meat market on the corner of Plum and West Main Street in downtown Carlinville. Frieda already knew the Paul family quite well, as two of the Paul daughters had married into the Ring family. They only dated a few months before Frank and Frieda were married on February 15, 1915. The couple owned their own market next to the Carlinville National Bank on the square for the next three years. Despite having a happy marriage and business, Frieda longed for something more exciting, and she greatly missed the theater. Her dreams gave birth to the Marvel Theater.

When the theater opened in 1920, Frieda became the face of the business and the music behind the curtain. She used her pianist skills to play music for silent films on a $10,000 pipe organ that the Pauls purchased for the theater. She organized and managed the shows and was always dressed to impress, bringing some glitz and glamour to Carlinville. Frieda was known for her passion and ambition for the Marvel and became a pioneer as one of the few women to have a prominent voice in business in the area. As you can imagine, it was uncommon to see a woman in authority in those days, but Freida wasn't shy or easily discouraged, despite some major setbacks.

What started out as a very average Thursday night in February 1925 turned into a terrifying ordeal for the Pauls. They closed the theater that night around 10:30 p.m. and headed home with about $180 from that night's profits. As they entered their home on South Broad Street, they were met by three armed masked men, who ordered them to put their hands up. Frieda was terrified not only for her and her husband but for their 10-year-old son, Norman. The men tied all of them up and snatched the $180 in theater money the Pauls had brought home, as well as about $1,000 worth of diamonds and

> **Use This Ticket and Save 20c**
> THIS TICKET and
> 30c admits two [2] adults
> 15c admits two [2] children
> TO THE
> **MARVEL THEATRE, Carlinville, Illinois**
> ON FRIDAY OF EACH WEEK
> except stage attractions and benefits
> GOOD UNTIL FURTHER NOTICE

AN UNUSED COUPON FROM THE EARLY DAYS AT THE MARVEL THEATER

other jewelry that belonged to Frieda. The robbers fled the home and left the Pauls in horror of how quickly their evening had turned into a nightmare.

After about 10 minutes, Frank was able to free himself and untie his family. Angry, Frank then jumped in the family vehicle and set out to find the assailants who terrorized his family. He searched all the way to Gillespie, about 14 miles away, before he realized he would likely never find the masked men. The robbers were never caught but Frieda didn't let fear control her life and she continued to run the theater she loved.

The next year, another tragedy occurred. On December 18, 1926, at around 3:00 am, crew from the Illinois Traction freight train discovered flames shooting out of both sides of the theater. Although the building was thought to be fireproof that sadly was not the case. Local firemen, as well as volunteers from the neighborhood, worked tirelessly into the early morning hours, dowsing the building with as much water as possible but the building eventually crumbled.

The fire also damaged the Reesor Wholesale Candy and Tobacco company building next door. Due to the intensity of the fire, the town was lucky more businesses were not damaged. Many suspected arson and foul play due to the rapid acceleration of the fire in multiple locations in the building, as well as the fact that three years before, the building suffered a much less severe mysterious fire. It was also odd that there were two similar

THE MARVEL THEATER IN 2018-YOU CAN STILL SEE THE MARVEL SIGN THAT WAS ADDED AFTER RE-BUILDING IN 1928.

theaters fires in the nearby towns of Gillespie and Highland around the same time. The police investigated but no one was ever arrested. The Pauls were left to pick up the pieces of their burned-out theater.

Freida and Frank were determined to keep the theater alive and assured the public they would rebuild the Marvel. Frieda immediately arranged to have the old opera house building cleaned and opened just in time for the folks of Carlinville to have a show the next evening. The Pauls spent the next two years, and roughly $70,000, rebuilding the Marvel. It re-opened on January 19, 1928, with the show "The Gay Retreat" and was better than ever. Frieda's impeccable taste made its way into the new Marvel with shiny glass doors, beautiful, not to mention comfortable, birch theater chairs, silk curtains, and a gorgeous chandelier adorned with 1,800 hanging crystals. The theater also included updated dressing rooms and an orchestra pit. Shortly after re-opening. the theater became one of the first in the area to feature movies with sound. The first talking picture was "The Jazz Singer."

In 1937, Frank passed away and while the theater had begun a partnership with the Frisina family in Taylorville, Frieda was still in charge and was the very active manager of the theater. Over the years, she continued to make sure the theater was updated with the latest technology, eventually adding air conditioning, advanced sound systems, and even built the Diana Drive-In in 1955, which operated west of town along Illinois Route 108 for many years. In 1977, the Marvel became a twin theater with 156 seats in the balcony and 300 seats on the main floor.

The beautiful and talented Frieda Paul passed away on June 8, 1976. Since her passing, those who have worked at the Marvel or have simply visited for a show, have come to believe that Frieda has never really left the theater. For her, the show must go on.

While conducting the *Haunted Carlinville Tours*, I have stopped by the Marvel Theater and told about its rich history. Over the last several years, I've had at least three separate occasions when someone on my tour had a story about Frieda. One woman said that she knew Frieda prior to her passing and had worked at the theater. She spoke of Frieda's outgoing personality and her love for the building. After Frieda passed, there would be times when she was alone in the concession area and out of the corner of her eye she would see a woman's face appear in glass. She would quickly turn around and see if anyone was standing there, causing a reflection, but would find herself alone. She was convinced it was Frieda.

Another past employee noticed odd occurrences near the old orchestra pit. She always hated being in there by herself and felt as though someone was watching her. It wasn't until she heard a phantom piano playing in the empty theater that she realized someone else was there -- they just weren't living. Others have reported seeing the curtains move when no air was flowing, as well as hearing footsteps in empty hallways.

Theaters are known to house the unexplained and I think the answer as to "why" has to do with all the energy that pours into them. Places like the Marvel not only featured films but they played host to musicians, actors, and performers of every kind, who made it their mission to entertain others. Every performance focused on lighting up the room with energy and I think some of that still remains, especially when it comes to Frieda Paul, who gave her heart to her precious Marvel Theater.

The Paul family no longer owns the Marvel Theater and it was most recently was bought by the Eisentraut family in 2015. You can still visit the Marvel today and if you look closely you can see the remnants of Frieda's passion in the small details of the building.

And, you never know -- you may just run into Frieda herself.

5. THIS OLD HAUNTED HOUSE

No matter where you are from, whether it be a large city or a small rural town, it's safe to assume you are aware of at least one supposedly haunted house in your neighborhood. Usually it's an old decrepit house that has been that reminds us of something you would find in a horror movie. But sometimes it's a seemingly normal house that for some reason sends chills down your spine. Owners of such houses are usually wary of talking about the unexplained, afraid of sounding crazy or tarnishing their home's reputation.

Even so, a good story always wants to be told and its hard to keep a good ghost story under wraps for long.

MILLIONAIRE'S ROW

Carlinville's "Millionaire's Row," located on East Main Street, showcases the town's wealth and prestige of years' past. The homes belonged to lawyers, businessmen, and politicians, many of whom left their imprint on Carlinville. Don "Burke" Denby, his wife, Vaughty, and their son, Tommy, lived a peaceful and privileged life on Millionaire's Row. The small family lived with Don's parents, John P. and Helen Denby. John was a successful local physician and helped provide a comfortable life for his son's young family.

On September 18, 1933, at around 5 o'clock in the evening, Tommy was playing on the rear porch of the family home. The porch had a shade which was often raised or lowered with a rope depending on how much sun the family wanted. Tommy was being his usual energetic self and while running around on the porch. he slipped and fell off the porch steps, catching his head in the loop of the shade rope. Several minutes later, the family realized that Tommy was not beside them and they went searching. As they reached the porch, they found the two-year-old's lifeless body hanging from the shade's rope. Tommy was rushed to the nearest hospital. The doctors tried everything to bring the little boy back, but it was too late. Tommy had broken his neck and could not be revived.

The toddler's death devastated the family and shocked the residents of Carlinville. The funeral was held several days later at the family home where the accident occurred. An exceptionally large group of sympathizers and mourners attended the child's funeral. Funeral services were conducted by Dr. W. M. Hudson, the President of Blackburn College. The solemn service had everyone sobbing as Mrs. Hudson sang, "Sometime We'll Understand." The boy's body was laid to rest in the Mayfield Memorial Park in Carlinville. His grave was marked with an assortment of floral arrangements from family, friends, and even complete strangers, all who grieved alongside the boy's parents.

Everyone wondered how this tragedy could have happened. Could it have been avoided? One young woman had these questions repeating over and over again in her head, having struggled with her feelings of guilt over the accident. The odd thing was, she was nowhere near the house when the accident occurred. This young woman was the family's nanny, who occasionally took care of Tommy. She had not been on duty that day. The night prior to Tommy's horrible accident, she woke up in the middle of the night, sweating from an unbelievable nightmare. She dreamt that Tommy was in some sort of danger at home and could be killed. The rawness of the emotions she felt during her nightmare disturbed her greatly. After some time, she was finally able to calm herself and fall back asleep.

She continued the next day as normal, having basically forgotten about the disturbing dream -- until news broke of little Tommy Denby's accident. The nanny wondered if she was given a premonition regarding the tragedy Tommy would face. For decades after Tommy's death, she was puzzled by her forewarning dream. Eventually, she told the story to family members who, in turn, shared the information with me. Was it truly a premonition or was it merely a coincidental dream? No one can say, but it certainly affected the rest of her life.

The Denby family did move forward in their lives after their great loss. Tommy's parents had three sons after his death and continued to live in the house where the accident occurred, filling it with love and laughter to help replace the sadness.

The house still stands on East Main street today. Numerous other children have lived in it over the years, running, playing, and skipping through the halls as any child would. However, there is one child who may have never left his childhood home -- Tommy Denby.

Rumors have persisted over the years that the young boy's spirit still inhabits the house. The sounds of tiny feet running around the house have been heard, along with a small shadow that flits about and adds a bit of mystery to the home. Whatever may or may not be present in the house, when

I hear stories about the spirit they all seem to be harmless and playful, just like you would expect from a little boy whose life was taken too soon.

CHARLES GILLMAN

Another home on "Millionaires Row" has gained a haunted reputation. Charles Gillman was one of the most influential people in Carlinville and his grandiose home made sure that people knew it. Charles was born in Brunswick, Germany, on May 4, 1843. His family immigrated to Carlinville in 1849, where they took up farming just north of the city. In 1872, Charles went into the dry goods business with local man Henry Johnson. The company was named Johnson and Gillman. After Henry Johnson's retirement, another man named Henry Chapino become involved in the business and the name was changed to Chapino and Gillman. The business would change names again when Henry Chapino died and Albert Mueller became involved. It was lastly known as Gillman and Mueller.

The same year that Charles started his business, he married Mary Hauer. They had five children, but unfortunately two would die in infancy, leaving three children surviving. Death would strike the family again in 1887, when his wife Mary passed away. Two years later, on February 6, 1889, Charles married Emma Breymann. Emma was young and vibrant, and more 15 years his junior, which led to even more Gillman children. Charles and Emma added four children to create their new blended family.

Charles's dry goods business was a great success and allowed him to not only support his family but also to become a well-respected business man. A staunch Democrat, Charles was known to have his fair share of opinions when it came to local politics. Luckily for Charles, his opinions became noticed and he was elected to represent his ward in the city council. In April 1897, his political aspirations rose again when he was elected Mayor of Carlinville. As mayor, he was passionate about bringing new businesses and projects to Carlinville, which gained him more friends than he could count. He held the mayoral position for two years and to prominent positions in the business world, such as director of the Carlinville National Bank.

At the turn of the last century, Charles seemed to have it all. He had a wonderful business, successful political career, and a doting family.

Unfortunately, he was plagued with a painful condition called Bright's disease, a type of kidney disease, causing pain, swelling, high blood pressure, and heart disease. Treatment in those days included warm baths, opium, cutting red meat, alcohol, and cheese from the diet, and even blood-letting. Patients could live years with Bright's Disease, until the kidneys shut down completely or they passed away from heart-related issues.

Charles lived with the disease until April 17, 1903, when his body could no longer fight, and he passed away. He was only a few days shy of his 60th birthday. His death was unexpected but at least it appeared as though he went peacefully while relaxing in his favorite chair. The Carlinville mayor, politician, businessman, and most importantly, family man was mourned by the entire town. A funeral service was held at his home on East Main Street. The number of people who arrived to pay their respects was so large that many had to stand outside the home because there simply wasn't any room inside. The casket was covered with beautiful roses and Easter lilies, making it apparent that Charles was a beloved man. He was then buried in the Lutheran Cemetery.

Charles' wife, Emma, and his children continued to live in the house on Millionaire's Row. As least two other Gillman family members passed away in the house. Leida Gillman, the daughter of Charles and Emma, died in 1926 at the young age of 31 from an unknown illness. The matriarch of the family, Emma Gillman, passed away 10 years later at the age of 76.

Other families have since lived in the home, but it was the Gillman family that made it such a prominent location in Carlinville. They were so proud of it that they have simply never stopped inhabiting the mansion.

One of the more widely-known ghost stories about the house has to do with strange lights. Neighbors and the occasional passerby have reported lights turning on and off in the house at times when the house was vacant. The lights didn't appear to be electrical mishaps but rather intentional events, turning on in one room, then off, and on in another room, as if someone or something was walking through the house turning on and off the lights.

Another strange account comes from a few years ago when the home was for sale. A woman went to look at the house and while standing in the kitchen, she heard footsteps above her. She ignored it at first, thinking it was her imagination. The footsteps continued and became even louder. Then it dawned on her that she was alone in the house. Out of curiosity, and the hope of reassuring herself that she wasn't crazy, she made her way upstairs. She thought she may find some sort of animal that had made the vacant house its home, which would at least mean she wasn't hearing things. As she approached the top of the stairs, the footsteps stopped. She searched high and low but no living being was found.

Baffled, she went back downstairs – only to have the lights suddenly start turning on and off in different rooms. Surely this couldn't be some sort of electrical mishap, right? The lights were fine when she first walked in the house but now they seemed to have a life of their own. She decided it was time to leave but then remembered yet again, she was all alone. She didn't want to leave all the lights on in the house, so she took a deep breath, mustered up some courage, and took out her phone to have someone on the other end to talk with as she went through the home and shut off all the lights. As the last light was turned off, she hurried out the door and returned to the comfort of her safe and non-haunted car.

CARLINVILLE'S MOST HAUNTED MANSION

The Anderson mansion, also known as the Macoupin County Historical Society home, sits on the edge of Carlinville and has been host to countless tours, festivals, and even weddings. Macoupin County locals also believe the property hosts a few lingering spirits from years past.

The history of the Anderson mansion begins with one of the most notable Carlinville citizens, Crittenden H. C. Anderson. Crittenden was born on January 26, 1819, in Christian County, Kentucky. He was the first born in a family of eight children. His father, Colonel James C. Anderson and mother, Ann, decided to move to Illinois when Crittenden was 16-years-old. The family arrived in Carlinville in October 1834. At that time, Carlinville was little more than a rough-hewn settlement, so the family quickly prepared a log cabin in which to survive the winter. The following spring, the family invested in 400 acres of Carlinville land, where they would setup their homestead. They began to farm and raised and sold livestock. Colonel Anderson also continued to invest in land, teaching his son the ins-and-outs of being a businessman. When Crittenden was 19, he officially became a business partner with his father and assisted him with buying and selling livestock, as well as driving cattle as far north as Michigan.

CRITTENDEN C. H. ANDERSON

On April 14, 1840, Crittenden married Mary Glass and the couple moved to a small farm that was gifted to them by Colonel Anderson. The couple had one child, James Henry Anderson, but, tragically, Mary died on May 4, 1841. Crittenden was overwhelmed. He couldn't believe that within a little over year, his young bride was dead, and he was the single father of an infant son. He moved back home with his parents and, while devastated by the tragic turn of events, he tried to move forward.

A little over 10 years after his first marriage, Crittenden married Mary Cole on November 14, 1850. Tragedy touched Crittenden again in August of 1851. Cholera swept through Carlinville, leaving behind a trail of death and despair. The fatal bacterial disease was especially cruel to the Anderson family. Crittenden's father, mother, brother, and sister-in-law, all passed away within a one-month span due to the terrible illness. After burying the dead and piecing his life back together again, Crittenden opened the first official drugstore in Carlinville with his brother-in-law, Dr. R. W. Glass. The drugstore, Anderson and Glass, opened on the northwest corner of the square. Along with another local man named William H. Rider, he built a three-story structure that known as the "Duplex Building." It became the first three-story building in the county and eventually the home of the Anderson family.

BANKING HOUSE OF C.H.C. ANDERSON IN THE LOOMIS HOUSE LOBBY, A LATER ENDEAVOR OF ANDERSON'S

Death found Crittenden again on January 20, 1857, taking his second wife, Mary. He was now left with two young sons to care for, including his only child with Mary, 3-year-old John C. Anderson. The year continued to bring misfortune for Crittenden. The drugstore housed one of the only safes in town and kept the money of many local businesses and citizens under lock and key. In 1857, the safe was stolen and taken into the street where it was blown up, exposing thousands of dollars in cash. The thieves escaped with the cash and Crittenden was left to cover the losses.

Whether due to true love, a lonely heart, or need for a mother to care for his sons, Crittenden married his third wife, Mary Stratton, only 10 months after his previous wife's death. With wife number three, he would have three more children. Their daughters Mary J. and Virginia wouldn't make it to adulthood, passing away at ages two and six respectively. Their only child to survive was their last born, Effie Anderson.

Crittenden left the drug store business in 1860 to return to his farming roots. Like remembering how to ride a bike, he regained his skills in buying and selling land and became known for his real-estate endeavors. In 1868, he opened an abstract and real estate office in the Chestnut and Dubois bank building. Two years later, he joined a bank under the name of Henderson Loan and Real Estate Association, which was operated by its president, George Holliday. In April of 1878, he went into the private banking business and opened the Banking House of C.H.C. Anderson in the lobby of the Loomis House Hotel on the square. The same year, the Chestnut & Dubois bank closed.

Crittenden had no knowledge that the neighboring bank was in such a dire situation. In fact, he didn't learn about the bank's closing until a note was posted on their building and the doors were locked. As you can imagine, the town went into a panic. People became worried about the safety and security of trusting their local banks, including the new Anderson bank. Some even speculated that the Anderson bank was involved in embezzling money. The former president of the Henderson Loan and Real Estate Association, George Holliday, had been accused of corruption and theft of funds used to build the new county courthouse, an issue that boiled the blood of all county residents. There were folks who thought Crittenden was in on the scheme, too.

On the day of Chestnut and Dubois' closing, Crittenden experienced a flood of concerned citizens who wanted to pull their money from his bank. Without skipping a beat, Crittenden remained calm and confident in his ability to sustain his banking business. At the end of the day he invited his depositors to come back to the bank and check his books for accuracy, vowing that he was an honest and competent banker. He remarked:

"Gentleman, I want you to understand that not only the assets of this corporation but every dollar of my private property is behind his bank."

Most of the depositors returned and found Crittenden to be a scrupulous banker that they could trust. His financial wisdom and savvy business sense created a successful Carlinville bank. In 1889, two of his children, John C. Anderson and Effie Anderson Mounts, became associated with their father's bank. That year, Crittenden became increasingly weak and suffered paralysis. On January 10, 1890, Crittenden died in the comfort of his home located on what is now the Macoupin County fairgrounds.

Prior to his passing, Crittenden gifted his son John C. with a large parcel of land. In 1883, John C. and his wife, Lucy, built a one-story residence on the property. By this time, John was working at his father's bank where he became very successful at growing the business. His young family also began to grow. In all, John C. and Lucy would have eight children, Jessie (b. 1881), John M. (b. 1883), Martha Rivers (b. 1884), Rivers McNeill (b. 1886), Luciel (b. 1888), Perry Boddie (b. 1892), James Crittenden (b. 1894), and Mary (b. 1897). All but the first three children were born in the family homestead that we know today as the Anderson Mansion.

As the family grew so did the house. In 1892, the Anderson family added a second story to their home. This is no small feat even today and most certainly was an architectural achievement in the late 1800s. John C. was still working as a banker in the family business and was becoming increasingly financially secure. The Italianate mansion boasted 13 rooms including a basement, attic, and gorgeous tower. Hand-carved wood features including an oak staircase and vestibule, eight unique fireplaces, and a large stained-glass window on the second-floor landing which was purchased at the World Columbian Exposition at the Chicago World's fair in 1893, created a magnificent

JOHN C. ANDERSON

THE ANDERSON MANSION IN 2018-TODAY THE HOME IS KNOWN FOR THEIR HISTORY TOURS, ESPECIALLY AROUND CHRISTMAS WHEN EACH ROOM IS DECORATED WITH A SPECIAL THEME.

home for the family. Perhaps the most impressive features were the indoor bathrooms, something that only the very rich would experience in this area at the turn of the twentieth century.

The family continued to live in the house for the remainder of their lives. The matriarch, Lucy Anderson, passed away on July 14, 1931. John C. continued to operate the bank until his death on July 5, 1932 at the age of 77. It wasn't long after this death that the bank was also put to rest. On March 6, newly elected President Franklin Roosevelt ordered Proclamation 2039, suspending all banking transactions effective immediately. This meant that nobody could deposit or withdraw money from their bank. Leading up to this decision, countless banks had failed. The Great Depression left Americans broke and mistrusting of banks. Americans began to pull their money out of banking institutions, which left a bank unable to sustain itself. Due to the failing banks, federal reserve banks were no longer able to hold onto gold reserves, equal to 40 percent of the paper currency, which was required. Faith in U.S. currency was dropping, and something had to be done. President Roosevelt's declaration placed all banking on hold until Congress could act and formulate a solution.

On March 9, 1933, the Emergency Banking Act of 1933 was passed. This act allowed 12 federal reserve banks to issue currency on good assets to the banks, so they could reopen and guarantee their depositors that their money was safe and insured. Americans no longer had the fear of their money going under with the bank and within a few weeks, over half of the money that had been withdrawn from banks was re-deposited. Most banks were able to reopen and return to normal. Unfortunately, C.H.C. Anderson was not one of them.

The Anderson bank was unable to retain its funds or make good on their depositor's assets. Those who had trusted the bank with their money were furious. Accusations of mismanagement and even embezzlement were made against the once-trusted institution. The bank was liquidated, and court proceedings began to resolve the debts and credits owed. By the end of 1934, 50 percent dividends were paid to the depositors amounting in $157,493.72. Even today, there are those who refuse to refer to the mansion on the fairgrounds as "Anderson Mansion," instead simply calling it "the mansion." Even though the bank has been closed for 85 years, there are families who continue to curse the Anderson name and blame the family for their misfortune.

After John C. Anderson's death, the home was left to his six living children. In 1940, the eldest Anderson child, Mrs. Jessie Claude Anderson Crawford, purchased the home from her brothers and sisters. Jessie lived in the house until 1973, when the Macoupin County Historical Society purchased the home and land. The mansion now operates as a museum with the land surrounding the home featuring several outbuildings that showcase early settlement life in Macoupin County. Those buildings include a blacksmith shop, saw mill, newspaper business, schoolhouse, and church.

Prior to the Macoupin County Historical Society's purchase of the property, the home sat in disrepair. Mrs. Crawford had been a widow for over 25 years prior to selling the property and was unable to keep up with the maintenance of such a large home by herself. In her last days of living in the home, Mrs. Crawford seldom left the house and became a shut-in. The lawn became overgrown, the roof and windows were in need of repair, and local teens had a habit of vandalizing the home.

It may have been the mansion's rough exterior that started the rumors of ghosts, but it would be first-hand, spooky experiences that would continue the rumors for future generations. In the late 1960s and early 1970s, children and teens began to tell stories of the haunted Anderson mansion. Teenagers would gather together late at night in front of the old house and tell ghost stories. Some would tell of a witch that lived in the home. She was said to capture children who entered her property and lock them in the basement. Of course, poor Mrs. Crawford was far from a witch but that didn't stop children from creating a scary twist to the old woman's presence.

Others spoke about a ghost with red glowing eyes. It was said that if you walked up to the house late at night you could see two red eyes peering back at you from the house's tower. Most who braved the house, to prove it was alive with spirits, would chicken out and run away before they stepped foot on the property. However, there were some that were determined to prove they were not afraid. Local teenagers started to dare one another to break into the house at night and steal something from the top floor. If they succeeded, they would get bragging rights and if they didn't, they would be branded a coward. As we all know, teenagers are not the most reasonable creatures and for some, the shame of being called a chicken was reason enough to break into a home. Teenagers began to steal items from the home, even when poor Mrs. Crawford was still living there! Some would steal books, wallpaper pieces, light bulbs, and virtually anything they could quickly grab that would prove they made it inside the haunted house. While in the midst of their thievery, the children would report hearing footsteps behind them when they were alone or even report seeing the ghost of Mr. Anderson himself. Personally, I think the bulk of these reports are due to a lot of adrenaline and a guilty conscience.

While most of the ghost stories are works of rascally teenagers with vivid imaginations, there were experiences noted within the home that led many to believe it was truly haunted. Once the historical society purchased the house, they went to work on repairs. Many times, there would be one or two volunteers alone in the home as they worked, either painting, cleaning, or repairing. Stories began to circulate that those volunteers would feel as though they were being watched. The feeling was never negative or ominous

SIDE VIEW OF THE ANDERSON MANSION

but rather curious, as if someone was just wanting to know what was happening to their home.

The mansion would eventually open for tours. Macoupin County schools arranged field trips to the mansion on a regular basis. My elementary school just so happened to be one of those schools. I remember touring the mansion when I was about 9-years-old. Even as a young child, I loved old buildings. I always imagined that I would one day grow up and live in a beautiful Victorian mansion. I'm still waiting for that dream to come true, but I have my fingers crossed. As we toured the home I remember coming upon a room upstairs that was surrounded by windows. This enclosed upstairs porch stopped me in my tracks. I remember feeling sick to my stomach. I didn't want to go in that room, but I couldn't understand why. That feeling stuck with me over the years and would often pop up again in my mind. Luckily on my next visit, I was at least able to answer as to why I was experiencing those feelings.

On my next tour of the mansion I was told about Martha Rivers Anderson. Martha was a beautiful and vibrant young woman. She was known to be incredibly intelligent, having attended Belmont College in Nashville,

MARTHA RIVERS ANDERSON

Tennessee and Virginia College in Roanoke, Virginia. After graduation she traveled abroad, looking to experience and learn new cultures. In 1913, she started working as a kindergarten teacher in South Dakota and then in North Carolina. She spent several years teaching and then returned home, where she became deeply involved in St. Paul's Episcopal Church and the Carlinville chapters of the Daughters of the American Revolution and Women's Club. Unfortunately, her active lifestyle would be put on hold when she contracted tuberculosis.

The disease is caused by an infectious bacterium that attacks the body, especially the lungs. Tuberculosis quickly became known as the "white plague." The disease attacked the lungs causing the patient to cough up white phlegm and labor their breathing. It was also called "consumption," due to the body being consumed by the disease causing the patient to lose weight and suffer from great fatigue.

Like many of those with tuberculosis, Martha sought out treatment after home remedies failed. In the fall of 1919, she spent some time at the Ottawa Tent Colony for consumption. The tented colony was located on the bluffs about a mile and half from Ottawa, Illinois. The facility was under the direction of Dr. James W. Pettit. The sanatorium was the second tent colony for tuberculosis treatment located east of the Mississippi. The first sanatorium was located 300 miles north of New York City near Saranac Lake. The Adirondack Cottage Sanitarium was opened in 1884 by Dr. Edward Trudeau and became one of the most widely-known locations for tuberculosis treatment. Dr. Trudeau knew the perils of tuberculosis, having suffered himself and losing a son to the disease. He believed it was the open air that helped him recover from the illness and he worked tirelessly on researching the disease and treating patients so that other might avoid the heartache that he endured.

In the first years of the next century, numerous other tuberculosis treatment facilities opened. The sanitoriums isolated the sick to help stop spread of the contagious disease. Every cough and sneeze meant a possible

OTTAWA TENT COLONY

death sentence for those living with tuberculosis patients. By 1900, tuberculosis was one of the three leading causes of death in America, with local newspapers reporting 9,000 deaths in Illinois annually. Everyone knew of someone who was burdened by the disease, many of whom would die.

Early treatment of the disease included an open-air environment. Patient beds would be placed on balconies or situated outside on a hill to allow the patients to breathe what they considered "cleaner" air. They would spend as much time outside as possible, even in the winter months. In fact, patients would often be seen outside in bed with snow falling around them. Due to the weight loss associated with tuberculosis, patients were fed a hardy diet to keep up their energy and slow their body from wasting away.

By the beginning of the twentieth century, doctors began to advise patients to stay away from northern states with cooler climates and seek treatment down south. Some speculated that the cold environment was detrimental to treatment. The Illinois State Medical Society set out to prove that Illinois climate was suitable to treat the disease and opened the Ottawa Tent Colony in 1904.

Martha Anderson's stay at the Ottawa Tent Colony likely included three dairy and fat rich meals a day, along with the required three quarts of milk and six raw eggs she would consume. She likely gained upwards of five pounds a week, the reported average for recovering patients at the colony. Martha most certainly spent most of her stay outside, including sleeping in the tented colony. She would be forbidden from intense exercise and even forced to limit her walking and talking, unless otherwise ordered by the doctor. Patients would refrain from close contact with one another and would be restricted from wandering the facility.

By 1911, the Ottawa Sanitarium reported that 91.5 percent of patients were discharged and able to return home. The Anderson family hoped Martha would be another one of their success stories. In September 1919, after several weeks of treatment, Martha returned home to the Anderson Mansion. She spent most of her time in the upstairs porch area. She followed the regimen of the Ottawa Tent Colony, hoping to be one of the lucky ones to beat the disease. She kept the porch windows open to allow the cool fall breeze to filter in and the Andersons made sure she ate well and stayed rested.

On February 21, 1920, at around 9:30 in the morning, Martha Rivers Anderson passed away in her bed on the Anderson mansion's upstairs porch. She was only 34-years-old. The family and Carlinville community mourned the death of the young woman, who at one point was filled with such life and promise. Martha's funeral was held at the Anderson mansion with people lining up outside to say good-bye to a woman who was greatly loved. She was then buried at the Carlinville City Cemetery. Mrs. Harry Miller of the Carlinville Women's club may have summarized Martha's passing the best, saying, "death lies on her like an untimely frost, upon the sweetest flower of the field."

VIEW OF THE UPSTAIRS PORCH WHERE MARY RIVERS ANDERSON PASSED AWAY

Martha made an impact on all of those she knew and continues to do so even today. In the upstairs porch area where Martha spent her last days, those who have toured the Anderson Mansion have reported feeling a sense of dread and depression, perhaps feeling the emotions experienced by the sick young woman. Others have reported hearing a woman talking softly in that area of the house, a voice almost sounding like a soft hum or whisper. When they went looking for the source of the noise, they realized there was nobody else upstairs. While walking down the hallway near the upstairs porch, people have reported seeing shadows move in the porch area. They would swear that someone must be in the room but when they go to investigate, they find it is empty. Martha left an impression on the Anderson Mansion and I think it's possible her energy still resides there today.

The attic of the mansion also offers some interesting and unexplained events, but they are likely not caused by Martha Anderson. In recent years, the attic of the Anderson Mansion has become home to a variety of military uniforms and memorabilia that have been graciously donated and loaned to the historical society. While touring the attic, you may encounter some unusual movement. Guests of the home have reported seeing the uniforms sway back and forth without anything visible causing their movement or a draft occurring. Whispers are also heard in the attic. Without a known reasonable source for the noises some have assumed it must be their imagination while others believe there is something paranormal occurring.

It's not just the attic that is full of antiques and history. The entire Anderson Mansion is filled with donated relics, some of which belonged to the Anderson family, but many that come from other Macoupin County citizens. Most, if not all, of the rooms are full, decorated and adorned with period specific items to highlight how our ancestors lived before us. Victorian dresses, antique toys, including a gorgeous dollhouse that I always admired, as well as bedding, and family portraits fill the rooms of the mansion. Those who have explored the home have reported seeing shadows move out of the corner of their eye, as well as the feeling of being watched, as they admire the antiques in the home. Maybe those feelings and experiences are associated with the items in the home, rather than the Anderson family themselves?

Haunted objects have long been a source of curiosity. Items such as the haunted "Robert the Doll" and the haunted Raggedy Ann Doll named "Annabelle" have made their way into museums and even turned into Hollywood gold, with movie adaptations raking in millions. There is even a traveling museum of the paranormal and occult that shuttles haunted objects from place to place so you can get an up close and personal view. Those who believe in the paranormal may want to explore the possibility that the hauntings of the Anderson Mansion may also be connected to the objects within its walls.

The basement of the home has also gained a haunted reputation. For generations local legend claimed the basement of the Anderson mansion was once a stop on the Underground Railroad. The story said that escaped slaves were once hidden there until they could be moved further north on the line to places like Springfield. Horrific tales of runaway slaves perishing in the

Underground Railroad hiding place beneath the Anderson Mansion lead many to believe that their spirits are still in the home.

Could such a story be true? Nope.

The Anderson mansion was constructed in 1883, almost two decades after the Civil War, when there was no longer a need for the Underground Railroad. Unbelievably, this is still one of the most popular rumors I hear when discussing local haunted history. It is also one of the easiest to discount.

But Underground Railroad station or not, the Anderson mansion continues to spark the imagination of those who visit. Whether you stop for a tour throughout the year or during one of the Macoupin County festivals hosted on the grounds, the mansion is an impressive building to visit with history and hauntings for all.

6. MACOUPIN COUNTY'S SECRET HELPERS

The Underground Railroad served as a network of people who assisted escaped slaves as they made their way north to freedom. After the slaves escaped, they would travel to a safe zone and receive food, shelter, and protection from "conductors," those who guided the escaped slaves, and "stationmasters," those who operated the safe zone. They would then travel to the next stop and repeat the process until they reached freedom.

The journey was full of danger and hardships. Travel happened at night, which left those on the Underground Railroad exposed to the wilderness with only the moonlight guiding them. Every step away from their former owner was crucial. If they got lost, left a trail behind, or were seen by anyone they risked being found and sent back to a life of slavery.

The Fugitive Slave Act of 1793 allowed the government to return runaway slaves to their owners and fine those who aided the slaves' escape. The penalties for assisting escaped slaves became even harsher with the Fugitive Slave Act of 1850. The new act compelled citizens to help return runaway slaves, even in free states where slavery wasn't allowed. Slaves were also denied the right to a jury trial and the penalties for assisting a slave or hampering their capture resulted in six months of jail time and a $1,000 fine (over $31,000 in today's dollars).

Due to the harshness of the Fugitive Slave Act of 1850, runaway slaves made it a priority to get as far north as possible, hoping to reach Canada and avoid the cruel laws of the United States. During this period, the Underground Railroad reached a peak with those trying to escape and those organizing safe stations. Macoupin County was home to several of these Underground Railroad locations during the years prior to the Civil War. Two of those homes belonged to the Braley Brothers.

Ellison Braley was born July 26, 1810, in Massachusetts. When he was 12-years-old, Ellison went to live with a man named Charles Valentine. Three years later, Ellison and Valentine went to Boston, where they became wholesale merchants. He spent the next several years traveling across Pennsylvania, Ohio and Indiana, selling goods. In 1839, Ellison made his way to Carlinville where he decided to stay, but not before returning to New York to marry Miss Catherine Coon on November 1, 1840. The couple returned to Carlinville, where he bought some land and started a small crop of corn and became involved in the tannery business. He remained in the tanning business for five years but eventually sold it to start a small store and later, operate a mill. Ellison went business with his brother, Philander, who also made his way to Carlinville, operating a new steam saw mill on Macoupin Creek. They took advantage of the Chicago and Alton Railroad's construction and obtained a contract to sell them railroad ties, which led to an amazing profit. Ellison and Philander eventually returned to farming and owned over 860 acres of land, making them some of the area's most successful farmers.

ELLISON BRALEY

The Braley family homes were located on East Main Street in Carlinville, next door to one another. Both men were abolitionists who strongly opposed slavery. Along with others in Macoupin County, the brothers risked prosecution in order to help slaves escape north. Ellison Braley was known to help transport runaway slaves in a wagon across Macoupin Creek, as well serve as a lookout for others carrying out the same task.

Philander Braley, born three years after Ellison, also helped those using the Underground Railroad. Richard Rowett, the son-in-law of Philander who became a Civil War General, gave a speech one night in 1880 and recalled a story told to him by his father-in-law. Referred to as "Uncle P," Philander was known to keep runaway slaves hidden in his home, usually just long enough for night to fall, when the slaves could move to the next station. One evening, the Braley family handyman, Pat, who was a stern Democrat, came into the hay loft to feed one of the horses. He was surprised to find Philander standing in the hay loft and insisting that Pat allow him to throw the hay and feed the horse. Pat was confused as to why his boss would offer to do all the work himself but figured he wouldn't argue with him and went on his way. As Pat exited the loft, Philander gave a sigh of relief. He was hiding runaway slaves under the hay in the loft. If Pat threw the hay himself, he would surely find the hidden runaways and expose his safe house on the Underground Railroad.

In 1999, *The Macoupin County Enquirer* newspaper printed interviews and letters from a member of a family that once owned the Philander Braley home. This person noted that the home contained a hidden small room in the cellar that had a small window that opened up to the area under the porch. The window was large enough for someone to crawl through it and into the secret room. One of the closets also seemed to contain a hiding place. While the closet seemed shallow, it extended in both directions. If you entered the closet, you could turn to the left and be completely hidden from the door. In the downstairs area, the family member recalled what appeared to be big built-in drawers that were really "wall beds.". The beds were flush against the wall but would pull down to open up a place to either sleep or hide. A friend of the family also noted there were panels in the stairway walls that had no knobs or handles but could be opened in order to hide runaway slaves.

Typically, slaves would cross over into the free state of Illinois through Alton. From Alton, they would make their way north through Madison county, crossing either into Macoupin County to go north towards Springfield or through Jersey County to head towards Jacksonville. From there, the former slaves would continue north until they felt safe or reached Canada, whichever came first.

Other Macoupin County stops on the Underground Railroad included the Dr. John P. Binney house outside of Staunton, near Silver Creek. Dr. Binney would hide slaves in his root cellar, feeding them fruit, eggs, and milk. The doctor was a valuable resource on the Underground Railroad due to his medical expertise. Injuries sustained while escaping the south were often untreated and could lead to serious injury or death. The Binney family was also a friend of Abraham Lincoln during his attorney years. Lincoln is thought to have visited the family home on numerous occasions. I'm sure their friend would have been proud of their resilience and strength against slavery.

Another stop included John Hart's home, about two miles northwest of Brighton. John was known to be a rough man who kept to himself. He would rarely talk to his neighbors or even engage in idle chat around town. Despite his hard exterior, John had strong convictions against slavery. His home became one of the Underground Railroad stops on the way to Carlinville.

John only had one close call during this period. One of the men he was helping on the Underground Railroad was caught and arrested. Even with the man in jail and John in trouble with the law, he didn't give up on helping the man reach his freedom. With the help of some like-minded citizens, John was able to distract the Brighton law enforcement and free the man from custody. The man eventually made it to Canada and John was never punished for his involvement in the Underground Railroad.

John Hart and the slave he assisted were some of the lucky ones on the Underground Railroad. Many weren't so lucky. Hefty rewards were constantly offered for those who returned runaway slaves to their owners or reported those involved in assisting.

A *Slave Report Book of 1841* documents reports of runaway slaves and published the following notice at the Macoupin County Courthouse:

"*$200.00 Reward- Ran off from the subscribers on Thursday morning, one Negro woman, named Rittea or Henrietta Jones, with her three children, Martha, Sarah, and James. The woman is large and fleshy, of a dark complexion and very sullen countenance; the oldest daughter Martha is six years old, the second Sarah is four, and the son James is two.*

The husband of Rittea Jones is a free dark mulatto about thirty-five years old, slightly spotted with small pox about 5 feet 8 or 9 inches high and quite impertinent when spoken to. Said Nicholas had a white man to carry his family to Carlinville, Illinois in a two-horse box wagon covered with white linen or cotton......"

JOHN FINNLY, St. Louis, MO.

Illinois was a free state but there were many southern sympathizers in the area that would report runaway slaves without hesitation. Even some of those who weren't in favor of slavery still had an issue with African-Americans living in their towns. When African-Americans arrived in Illinois they not only had to worry about being arrested for escaping from slavery but also finding a place to call home.

In 1844, a slaveholder from Missouri released 15 slaves. They boarded a boat and set out for Alton, Illinois, however, when they landed on shore the Alton citizens refused to let them stay. Their arrival was seven years after the murder of abolitionist Elijah Lovejoy and racial tensions were still high.

The former slaves were taken to the river and told to follow the mouth of the Piasa Creek nearby. They made their way to the area that is now the village of Piasa and settled, becoming some of the first former slaves to acquire land in Macoupin County.

As the country entered into the Civil War in 1861, the Underground Railroad system began to slow but the discussion over slavery heated up. Abolitionists became increasingly involved in local politics and many gladly offered their services to the Union cause. One of the most influential abolitionists in Macoupin County was John M. Palmer.

FRIENDS IN HIGH PLACES
HISTORY AND HAUNTINGS OF JOHN PALMER

There are several notable homes in Carlinville. Some are known for their unique architecture, some for their upscale features, and others are known for the residents that once called them home. Located at 305 South East Street, you will find the Palmer House. John McAuley Palmer built the home in late 1840s and became one of Carlinville's most prominent citizens.

He was born September 13, 1817, in Kentucky to Louis and Ann Palmer. His family made a modest living making cabinets and eventually decided to try farming for a living, moving to Illinois in 1831. The Palmers were progressive for a family in the early 1800s. They were practicing Jefferson Democrats who opposed slavery and encouraged their children to receive formal education. In fact, both John Palmer and his brother Elihu attended college in Alton, Illinois. One thing about college in the 1800s that still rings true today is the price. College wasn't cheap, and the Palmer family wasn't wealthy. John and Elihu worked their way through college, performing janitorial work at the school and manual labor to make their college payments.

In 1836, an ambitious John became interested in the Texas Revolution and decided to join a group called the "Revolutionists" from St. Louis. The plan was to travel downriver and make their way to the Texas battlefield. The night before leaving, John was stopped by a police officer in Alton who handed him a piece of paper that can only be described as a warrant. The paper stated that John M. Palmer was to be detained for debts owed. Shocked, John asked the officer how he could avoid being detained. The officer agreed to accept $4.50 and $1.25 payments to avoid imprisonment. John only had $2 to his name but pleaded with the officer and was allowed to make the rest of the payment the next day. At any rate, the trip down south to Texas never happened. Now broke, John was forced to drop out of college.

In 1837, John met a man named C. N. Henderson of Connecticut who was in the clock business. John had previously boarded with some men who also sold clocks for a living and he decided to take on the occupation of salesman. John realized that he was also a talented craftsman and began to learn how to

JOHN M. PALMER

manufacture clocks. Clock making became a large part of John's life and he became an intricate part of the Henderson Company.

A nimble hand for clock making allowed John to save some money and he decided to return to college and pursue law. Between college and selling clocks, John finally felt like he was making progress. In the meantime, his brother Elihu had married and began the life of a Baptist pastor in Carlinville. Elihu convinced John to take a position at the law office of John S. Greathouse, which set John up for a new life in Carlinville.

It didn't take long for John to learn the politics of the area and catch the eye of local Democrats, who persuaded him to make a bid for county clerk. Although he lost the election, he made an impression on county officials. They were so impressed with him that soon, after the election, John, without even passing the Illinois bar, was allowed to represent a defendant in an assault case. Even without a proper law degree, John won the case and began the reputation of a competent and talented attorney.

In December of 1839, John made his way to Springfield to apply for his law license. While in Springfield, John met an old friend and made a new one. A year prior to arriving in Springfield, John and a friend were making the rounds selling clocks. They stopped off one night in Hancock County and reserved a room to rest for the evening. During the night, a loud bang woke the two men and they were greeted by the inn keeper and two other gentlemen. In an awkward exchange, the inn keeper stated that John and his friend would be sharing the beds with the other two gentlemen as the inn was full and they needed somewhere to stay. One of his new bedmates was a rather tall man who asked John about his politics. John stated that he was a Democrat and his friend was a Whig. The other stranger, who was notably short, remarked that he would bunk with John, the Democrat. That short man was none other than Stephen A. Douglas and the tall man John T.

Stewart. After a night of what could have been very uncomfortable accommodations, the men parted as friends.

It was Mr. Douglas to whom John would submit his law license application in Springfield. It's hard to deny the dreams of someone who shared your bed and in a less awkward exchange, Stephen Douglas was happy to grant the license. John spent the day in Springfield and stumbled upon a crowd that had gathered to listen to the speech of a rather tall and gangly man. The speech was captivating and left John wanting more. The next day before John left Springfield, he met the gentleman who gave the impressive speech. His name was Abraham Lincoln.

STEPHEN A. DOUGLAS

Carlinville now had a new licensed attorney in town. While John wasn't very experienced he was able to tell a story unlike anyone else. In the end, that's what a good lawyer does -- they tell the story from their client's perspective and with a little razzle-dazzle and charm, they can command a court room.

In 1843, a year after his marriage to Melinda Ann Neeley, John became an important member of the local Democratic party and was elected Probate Judge of Macoupin County. Things were good for the Palmers and they quickly became a prominent family in Carlinville.

Now that John had tackled the law and dipped his toes in politics, it was now time for him to rise to fame in the military. During the Mexican-American war, John was elected captain of his company and a member of the Constitutional Convention. He began to realize some of his ideas were rather unpopular. John was outspoken against slavery and found many of his beliefs met with opposition. In 1851, he was elected to the State Senate and continued to speak out against slavery, while carefully balancing his role as a Democrat.

The Missouri Compromise repeal of 1854 (Kansas-Nebraska Act) further tested John's Democratic loyalties. The repeal, which was strongly promoted by John's old friend Stephen Douglas, created the Kansas and Nebraska territories and allowed them to determine their own stance on slavery.

Abolitionists became concerned about the expansion of slavery. Troubled over the act, John then announced himself as an Independent Democrat. The congressional tension between the different parties was reflected in the relationship between John and Stephen Douglas. The two men were now in different political factions and their friendship cooled dramatically.

In contrast, John's new politics brought him closer to his Springfield friend, Abe Lincoln, who knew John was struggling with his stance on the matter. "You have a strong struggle with yourself, and you have determined not to swallow the wrong," Lincoln wrote in a letter to John Palmer that was dated September 7, 1854.

It became obvious that Lincoln had faith in Palmer. When writing to Alexander Morean, a Whig politician in Jerseyville, Lincoln encouraged him to find someone to make a speech against the Kansas-Nebraska act, stating "Palmer is the best if you can get him."

In 1856, John became the president of the Illinois Republican Convention and worked closely with Lincoln. Unfortunately, the Republican presidential candidate, John C. Fremont, didn't win and Democrat James Buchanan took office. While the Republicans didn't make it to the White House for that term, John and Abraham were fired up and ready to take on the Democrats closer to home.

In 1858, the great debates between John's two friends began. Abraham Lincoln, the Whig turned Republican, took on Stephen Douglas, the Democrat, for the position of United States Senator from Illinois. Lincoln and Douglas had long been friends and John was mixed up between them. They had several awkward encounters as John campaigned for Lincoln.

Lincoln lost the election, but two years later, he would win much higher office and became the President of the United States. Unfortunately, the country was tearing itself apart and on its way to war.

When Lincoln put out a call for troops, John became a Colonel in the 14th Regiment Illinois Volunteers. He was later promoted to the rank of Major General. His reputation as a commander was cemented after his victory at the battle of Farmington where he used the swampy woods to his advantage and routed the Confederates. Eventually, John clashed with General William T. Sherman and he resigned his commission in August 1864.

But Lincoln refused to accept it. He called John to Washington and made him the Commander of the Department of Kentucky, which oversaw law and order in a state filled with Confederate deserters, dysfunctional army units, and chaos in the streets.

This time in John's military service may have been the most difficult. The towns were filled violence, mayhem, and escaped slaves trying to find freedom. John took it upon himself to ensure those escaping would find refuge in the Union camps and even issued an order requiring carriers to support transport for the former slaves and get them to safety as well, as help them seek employment and self-sustainability. His plans were noble but hated by the people he was overseeing. In fact, he was sued for over $70,000 by slave owners who claimed he aided the escape of their property.

This wasn't the first time John faced legal troubles due to his convictions. After his success in the battle of Farmington, he was sent home for a period due to illness. He brought a young black man named Martin Taylor with him to Carlinville. The Palmer family stated Martin was employed as a personal attendant for John. When it was time for John to return to the war, Martin stayed behind with the family. Rumors began to spread that John helped Martin escape from slavery and his family was harboring him in Carlinville. While John was away, his family was awakened by the sound of banging and commotion on the front door. Local legend says John's daughter, Elizabeth, took matters into her own hands and rushed downstairs to find a group of southern sympathizers outside. The gang was planning harass the family of a Union general, but they weren't prepared for Elizabeth. She opened the door brandishing a pistol and swearing to shoot first and ask questions later, the gang retreated into the night.

While the family avoided the violence of the southern sympathizers, they had other issues brewing. In December of 1862, a Macoupin County grand jury charged John with violating the Fugitive Slave Law. Due to lack of evidence that Martin Taylor was ever a slave, the Palmer family was found not guilty.

In 1865, formal charges were again brought against John Palmer for his efforts in Kentucky. In December of that year, Alabama adopted the Constitutional Amendment prohibiting slavery, giving the amendment precedence and validity. By the time John faced the charges, the laws had changed and all counts against him were dropped.

He returned home to Carlinville on May 1, 1866 with a reputation for bravery and justice. In April 1867, John and his family moved to Springfield where he was eventually elected Illinois Governor.

Even though John left Carlinville, he remained tied to the community and became the talk of the town yet again in 1869. During the building of the current Macoupin County Courthouse, citizens and county officials were disagreeing on spending. The budget had soared far beyond what the citizens were originally told, and they petitioned the state government to put a stop to it. County officials relied on their former colleague, Governor John Palmer, to help the passage of legislation that would allow them to continue borrowing money and complete the courthouse, regardless of citizen approval. Governor Palmer took some heat for his support of the legislation and the once-beloved Carlinville citizen gained new enemies in his former hometown. The *Chicago Inter Ocean* newspaper reported that former supporters of Palmer now believed he "outraged common decency and sold his honor for a fat fee."

John's legal skills were needed again when he became the attorney for several of the bond holders and county commissioners, appearing in court and threatening fines and legal action against naysayers of the bonds. Once again, he caused more controversy in Macoupin County.

Despite losing some of his local popularity, John was elected to the U.S. Senate in 1890 as a Democrat, returning to his old political party. He briefly considered a run for president in 1896 but ultimately decided against it.

John M. Palmer died just four years later on September 25, 1900. Palmer's home in Carlinville soon became a landmark as a location visited by Abraham Lincoln.

In addition to holding a claim to Lincoln fame, the home has gained a reputation for inhabiting the spirits of past residents. During *the Haunted Carlinville Tours*, I would often be asked if the Palmer house was haunted. On

THE JOHN PALMER HOUSE TODAY

more than one occasion I would have someone else on the tour chime in about hearing rumblings of the house feeling eerie and strange noises occurring inside.

In the home's more recent history, it was put on the market for sale and an open house was held. I take the term "open house" seriously and know they will let even the strangest of people come and take a peek at the home, myself included. Upon arrival, it was obvious the home had seen better days. The home was only about half of the size of the house it once was. John Palmer literally cut off a portion of his home to give to his daughter for a wedding present -- not a shabby wedding gift if you ask me.

One of the interesting things about standard ghost hunting equipment, such as a meter that measures electromagnetic fields, is that a lot of people use similar equipment when they consider purchasing a home to check the wiring and other sources of electrical energy in the home. This made it perfectly legit -- in my opinion -- to bring one along for an open house.

I toured the home and found it to be rather uneventful. I didn't have any creepy feelings or negative vibes. There was a spike in the EMF in the downstairs closet as well, where I also experienced a cell phone malfunction, but there was nothing significant. The only other place that I wanted to explore was the basement. The basement is only accessible through an outside door that when opened, was covered in cave crickets. Have you ever seen a cave cricket? If not, Google it and be prepared for nightmares.

Unlike the rest of the home, the basement yielded some unexplained occurrences. An initial EMF reading was unremarkable with little to no EMF present, even near the electrical box. As I moved closer to the back of the basement I noticed a hole in the foundation and as I approached the opening, and asked out loud what it was, the EMF spiked to "red" on the meter, signaling a high electromagnetic field disruption.

I continued to move towards the opening and the EMF continued to stay "red." The opening, or hole, in the foundation appeared to lead to a tunnel. There were newer wooden beams along the top of the tunnel, but the foundation appeared to be original, perhaps limestone. The tunnel was long and approximately three-feet-high. I had no idea how far it went back. There was a cool draft coming from the tunnel, which I couldn't help but notice since it was about 90-degrees outside. There was no other draft or breeze in any other part of the basement. The EMF continued to be high and the feeling that I wasn't alone was obvious.

As I got closer, I heard a loud shuffling in the tunnel, however I could see nothing in there by the light of the flashlight that I had with me. The noise lasted for a few seconds and sounded like someone crawling on their hands and knees, leading me to back away from the opening. Whatever was making the sound, I didn't see it.

The question is -- what is the opening/tunnel for? I'm not a structural engineer but I can tell you that it appeared to have no purpose and I couldn't see where the tunnel led. Also, the home was built in the late 1840s and a crawlspace would not have been used for electrical or plumbing hookups.

One theory is the tunnel connects to an outdate dated sewer system. Another more interesting theory is that the tunnel leads somewhere outside and was a part of the Underground Railroad. I have no evidence to prove it, but we know the Palmer family supported the freedom of slaves and assisted at least one young African-American man in escaping the south.

Of course, it may just be a boring old leftover tunnel with no real purpose, but then what did I hear that day? What spiked the EMF? What made my hair stand on end?

The Palmers may no longer inhabit their old house but perhaps someone else still does.

7. THE COUNTY CREATURE

Unexplained phenomenon and things that go bump in the night are not confined to old buildings. In fact, some of the scariest and most unnerving experiences take place outside. About five years ago, I was chatting with a group of people about strange area history when one of them mentioned something that had me both confused and intrigued. They spoke of a creature that was rumored to inhabit Macoupin County. The creature has worldwide notoriety and has been tirelessly debated for centuries. It goes by many different names, but in the Midwest, we more commonly know it has Bigfoot. Yes, I am talking about THE bigfoot.

My only real knowledge of bigfoot came from the 1987 family movie *Harry and the Hendersons*, as well as occasionally turning on a random television show about the subject. Needless to say, I didn't take the idea of Bigfoot seriously and most certainly didn't expect to hear that one may be living right here amongst us in Macoupin County.

This conversation was the first I'd heard of Bigfoot in the area, but I soon found out that its presence was more widely-known than I thought. I began to ask some older citizens about the idea of a giant hairy ape inhabiting Macoupin County. Of course, I had to approach the subject lightly and was a bit hesitant to bring up such a strange idea. The response was surprising. Several people were aware of the alleged Bigfoot presence and some even had their own stories.

One man told me about an experience he had near Gillespie Lake. He said he was out near the lake and was heading home from hunting when he heard a strange cry that almost sounded like a grunt. He knew the sound wasn't a coyote and it sure didn't sound human. It startled him, and he began to walk a little quicker. The man eventually made it safely back home, but he couldn't shake the feeling that he was being watched by an unknown creature in the woods.

Once I started looking, tales of a creature lurking in Macoupin County wilderness were not in short supply. Perhaps the most widely reported account occurred in December 1936. Every day, 14-year-old Lenora Rhoads would return from home from Carlinville High School the exact same way. She would catch the bus with her friends after school and ride it all the way to Plainview, near Macoupin Station. Lenora and her friends would then walk together the rest of the way home, except for the last half-mile, which Lenora would walk by herself. She barely gave the walk a second thought, having completed it every day, over and over again. That is, until something made her take notice of being all alone.

During one week in mid-December 1936, as Lenora walked that last stretch of road by herself, she began to hear what she described as "guttural mutterings," which ended with a shrieking scream. Lenora was incredibly rattled by the unsettling noises but tried to convince herself that perhaps it was her imagination or just a strange animal. All hopes of ignoring the strange grunts disappeared on December 15 when the source of the strange noise made an appearance.

As Lenora was walking, she realized the primitive noises were getting louder. She began to pick up her pace, trying to reach home as quickly as possible, while ignoring her increasing heart rate and the panic that was rising in her chest. Suddenly, a tall, imposing figure, covered in matted hair, emerged from a patch of weeds on the side of the road. Lenora ran as fast as her legs could carry her to the nearest neighbor, where she recounted her terrifying ordeal. The neighbor contacted Sheriff A.S. Henry, who immediately came out to investigate.

The sheriff questioned area residents to see if they noticed anything strange recently. One local man said that he had witnessed an "ape-like figure" in nearby underbrush. Even with what appeared to be a corroborating report, authorities were understandably skeptical of the "ape-man" theory, especially considering the film *Tarzan Escapes* had recently show in the local theater. Many thought the sightings were nothing more than a vivid imagination.

Police also questioned Carlinville student Joseph Liston, who traveled the same road as Lenora to get home. Joseph reported that he never heard any grunting or screaming on his way home, although it should be noted that Joseph traveled the road at a slightly different time than Lenora.

James Rhoades, Lenora's father, had originally discounted his daughter's claims of strange noises on the walk home. He figured it must have been an owl or some other creature. However, when he heard about his daughter's recent close encounter, he was determined to find the person, or creature, responsible for scaring his little girl.

It should be noted that this was not the first time the family had a run in with a mysterious entity. Some time prior to Lenora's experience, the family was driving down a road near their home and Mrs. Rhoads pointed out a shadowy figure on the side of the road. Mr. Rhoads assumed it was someone trying to steal from their fur business nearby, so once his family was safe at home, he returned to the spot where the shadowy figure was seen with a shotgun. Whoever, or whatever, Mrs. Rhoads had seen, the figure was gone.

This time, Mr. Rhoads concocted a plan that would use Lenora as bait. Lenora would walk home from school just as she had always done, but this time an armed posse would be following her and prepared to capture the perpetrator. Unfortunately, Lenora was too frightened to participate, and the plan was called off.

Area residents went out on their own search of the woods, trying to see if there was any sign of the ape-man or anything else that might be stalking the area. The search turned up nothing.

That didn't stop fear from continuing to build in the community and children became increasingly terrified of walking alone. Children and teens came up with their own theories as to the ape-man's identity. A story began to circulate that the creature was a killer who viciously murdered two young boys 17 years before. The killer placed the boy's bodies on a barbed wire fence, the story claimed, and positioned them like scarecrows. Now, the killer was back!

A more reasonable, and yet still unsettling, theory evolved. The police believed the figure seen was not an ape-man or a child killer, but rather of an escaped mental patient. Six weeks before, two men escaped from the Alton State Mental Hospital and had been on the run ever since. The men were described as being about 5'10 and appearing unkempt. Both patients were mentally disturbed and may have been prone to uncontrolled grunting and piercing screams.

The following month, a 35-year-old man named Elmer Morris, a fur trapper, was arrested in Alton on a charge of robbing John Rosentree, a local Macoupin Station farmer. Morris was recently paroled from state prison and local authorities believed he may have been involved in additional robberies. Some believed he was the elusive "ape-man." Morris was a tall, and rather hairy fellow, who had a crippled arm, which he held in an odd position and another arm that was much longer and hung low. It was possible, they said, that Leonora mistook the thief for a wild creature.

The identity of whatever was being seen in the area may never be certain, although with all the possibilities, I personally think there is an explanation other than Bigfoot. Lenora's ape-man sighting was just one of many that have occurred in the area over the years. A simple search of online message boards regarding Bigfoot and other hominid creatures will result in numerous stories of locals reporting the beast.

One story from 1978 recalls the experiences of a young man and his girlfriend. They were about 13 miles south of Carlinville, and 10 miles west of Gillespie, when they decided to park their car in a remote spot near some woods at the edge of farmer's field. They climbed into the backset to "make out" but suddenly, a foul odor engulfed the car. The stench was followed by a piercing scream and what the young man described as "several low tone grunts." The couple could tell that whatever was making that smell and screech was nearby. Deciding not to take their chances with whatever was out there, the couple quickly put on their clothes and drove away. The young couple's passion may have been interrupted but at least they left with an interesting story.

There is one particular location near Carlinville that has been the source of several Bigfoot sightings. Off Highway 108, outside of town, there is a little community called Hagaman, which is also known as Hagaman Bottoms. It constantly turns up in area Bigfoot accounts. A motorist shared a story that occurred there a few years ago when he was approaching a hill in the area. He saw a 7-8-foot reddish-brown creature crossing the highway in front of him. It was a little after 5:00 p.m. and while it was starting to get dark outside, he had no doubt of about what he saw.

Another report dates to 1989 when a young woman was driving home after her shift at the Carlinville McDonalds. She recalled that it was probably after 1:00 a.m. when she approached the bridge at Hagaman Bottoms. Her headlights revealed a tall, dark figure next to the road. Understandably, she became incredibly unnerved and accelerated her car. Just as she passed it, the creature reached out its hand towards her vehicle. I'm sure she let out a sigh of relief once she reached her destination.

Additional reports of a tall dark figure near the tree line have been reported in the Macoupin County towns of Bunker Hill, Girard, Hettick, Plainview, and Shipman. Even with the countless reports of a Bigfoot-type of creature in the area, not to mention thousands more around the country, verified evidence of its existence still hasn't been found. Sure, you will find people who swear they have a piece of Bigfoot hair or the oddly desired bigfoot scat, but the reality is, there is nothing that has convinced the scientific community, or even the general public, that Bigfoots is real. If they exist, then why haven't we found a bigfoot carcass? Why hasn't someone trapped one in the wild, or provided another piece of physical evidence? Besides the belief that Bigfoot is a myth, there are also some pretty unconventional theories that may explain why the existence of Bigfoot is so difficult to prove.

Some believe that Bigfoot is actually a supernatural being. In fact, Native Americans spoke of the Wendigo, or "the evil spirit that devours man," long before settlers arrived in America. This spirit was said to be up to 15-feet-tall with glowing eyes, fangs, and covered in matted hair. It was believed that the spirit was once human but was created when the human engaged in cannibalism. The Wendigo would prowl for someone to crave its insatiable hunger, traveling the wilderness until it could find someone to snatch up and devour.

In more recent history, the idea that Bigfoot is a ghost has created a bit of a buzz in the paranormal field. Some believe that Bigfoot might have been a creature that existed at one point in history, perhaps a type of evolutionary crossover hybrid between man and ape. They believe this creature's spirit still lingers, as would any other ghostly apparition that people more commonly reference. Just like with any other ghost you might experience, a Bigfoot spirit might give off a certain odor, make sounds, or appear as an apparition.

Others believe that Bigfoot is an inter-dimensional entity. One idea regarding the inter-dimensional theory is based in Lorentzian traversable wormholes, which some believe act as portals to allow things to travel to and from other universes. They believe Bigfoot may actually be from another universe -- either within our own, like an alternate dimension/timeline (think *Back to the Future*) or some other universe completely different than ours. It's complicated to say the least and based completely on "what ifs." I sure do wish I had Doc Brown to explain this to me. He made time travel seem so easy.

Do you like aliens? Believe it or not there is a Bigfoot theory for you, too. Theories persist that Bigfoot sightings are related to UFOs. Cryptozoologists, those who study creatures in folklore, have noticed a correlation between UFO sightings and bigfoot sightings. They also cite stories such as that of Reafa Heitfield. In 1973, Reafa was living in Cincinnati, Ohio. She woke one night at around 2:30 a.m. to get a drink of water. She made her way to the kitchen and noticed something strange outside the kitchen window. She could see a bright cone of light and when she looked at the source of the light, she saw ape-like creatures, grayish in color, walking towards the light and then disappearing. Maybe Bigfoot is just an overgrown version of *Alf*?

You can see that when it comes to Bigfoot there may be just as many theories as to how it exists as there are reports of its existence. Personally, I find it hard to believe that a living, breathing, ape-man is living out in the woods but has never been verified. Still, it's hard to discount all the sightings and unexplained events that lead those to believe in Bigfoot's existence. Until proven otherwise I think I will remain a skeptic but I invite all those interested in finding the ape-man to look no further than Macoupin County.

Bigfoot might be closer than we think.

8. MACOUPIN MONEY MAKERS

Are we there yet? There are likely few questions that provide more annoyance than this phrase. For those in Macoupin County's early days, travel was not a leisurely activity. Until the 1850s, most of the area was stuck with a horse and buggy for travel. In 1852, the Chicago and Alton Railroad was completed, finishing a track from Alton to Springfield. The process of building the railroad led to an influx of job opportunities in Macoupin County, with several towns in the area gaining a train station. Carlinville was one of those towns.

The railroad industry quickly became a revenue source for Macoupin County. The railroad was booming and towns like Carlinville soon became known for their stations. Trains made travel easier and more and more people were able to travel to Carlinville and conduct business. However, it wasn't all peaches and cream. Little towns like Carlinville were no longer isolated and some of those who entered were up to no good. Train stations became known as somewhat dangerous places. Robberies began to occur on the trains, as well as at the station, with thieves targeting unsuspecting passengers.

It was shortly after midnight on May 1, 1895, when engineer Frank Holmes boarded the train known as the St. Louis Night Express. He was in route to Carlinville and set to arrive a little after 11:00 a.m. A few miles north of Carlinville, the Chicago and Alton Railroad track he was riding crossed with the Jacksonville Southeastern Railroad, requiring him to slow down the train and wait for a signal to cross. As Frank's train came to a stop, three men boarded the cab of the engine. They immediately began shooting. Frank was shot. One of the other men on the train, Frank Tuggle, was able to escape the engine and run to Carlinville for help. A mail clerk on board heard the shots and ran to the rescue, even firing a shot at one of the assailants. The robber was struck, and the mail clerk was able to apprehend him. The other two murderers escaped.

Eventually all three of the train robbers -- Edward Bryant, Jack Frost, and Benjamin Myers -- were found and taken to the Macoupin County Jail.

CARLINVILLE TRAIN STATION IN THE EARLY 1900S

Edwards Bryant and Jack Frost confessed they were on their way to Kansas City when they stopped in Carlinville to visit with Jack Frost's relatives. While in town, they met Myers. They said it was Myers who convinced them that robbing a train was a good idea. They put their plan into action and boarded the train while it was stopped. Myers instructed the two men to get to the engineer and get him to surrender the train. The men did as he instructed and approached the engine. When they arrived, they ordered both Frank Holmes and Frank Tuggle to put their hands up. Frank Holmes was in a stooping position and when he stood up, Frost fired. Frost said he was startled by Frank Holmes and that is why he shot him. He never planned on killing anyone. After the incident, Myers was able to escape but was arrested later in Carlinville. All three men were sentenced to serve prison terms in Joliet prison.

The railroad continued to expand and by the early 1900s, a new rail system of trolleys became a fixture in Macoupin County towns. The new transportation yet again provided area citizens with employment opportunities and helped boost the downtowns of Macoupin County. Sadly, in October of 1910, the increasingly popular form of transportation was responsible for one of the worst tragedies in Macoupin County.

Thirty-six people were killed when two trolley cars collided head-on in Staunton, about 20 miles south of Carlinville. Both trains were headed to fairs, one in St. Louis and one in Springfield. The No. 14 trolley had orders to stop at two places in Staunton. The motorman, John Liermann, followed orders for the first stop but missed the second. At Dickerson's curve, a couple miles from Staunton, the two trolleys crashed head-on, having no time to slow down or veer off the track. Both motormen realized what was about to happen and jumped from the trolley cars, surprisingly receiving only a few bruises. The crash was brutal, and the dead were scattered. Many people received horrific injuries leading to amputations and serious surgeries. Those who died were taken to Carlinville. Of the 36 that perished, nine were mangled so badly that identification was impossible.

John Liermann eventually admitted responsibility for the tragedy. The inquest into the accident noted Liermann's carelessness but stated he was of clear mind when the crash occurred.

The county's worst trolley crash was just an accident.

COAL COUNTY

There was another industry that proved both valuable and deadly to the area. During the town's early formation, Carlinville citizens relied heavily on the area's natural resources for their livelihood. Farming was crucial, not only to supply a family's food, but also to be used for trade. The area timber built their houses and also became a valuable resource to sell to industries, such as railroad companies. The area around Carlinville, soon to be known as Macoupin County, was rich in opportunity for those who were willing to get their hands dirty. One of their most widely sought-after resources was perhaps the dirtiest. Coal, or black diamonds as some would call it, became crucial to local economy. In fact, Macoupin County has long been known as "Coal County" and with that title there is a sense of hard work and determination that follows.

Coal mines in Macoupin County began popping up in the late 1860s. One of the first was located in Girard in 1867. Another opened three years later in Carlinville. About 19 miles north of Carlinville, you will find the town of Virden. Like several other Macoupin County towns, Virden relied heavily on coal mining for its economy and sustainability of its citizens. It was in Virden that one of the bloodiest mining disputes in American history occurred – still known today as the "Virden Massacre."

By the 1890s, organized unions were gaining popularity, especially with miners who were tired of the dwindling wage and grueling demands of the job. Miners began to walk off the job and go from town to town to rally support for their unionization. By 1897, an outpouring of miners, including those from the Virden mine, had joined the United Mine Workers Union. Almost immediately following the miner's agreement with the union, mine operators, including The Chicago-Virden Coal Company, which was the largest coal company in the state, refused to pay miners the union wage they agreed upon.

The miners were steadfast in their refusal to work for anything less than the agreed-upon wage. The coal company responded in the spring of 1898 by recruiting African-American workers from southern states to act as strike breakers. The idea was that the miners would see the African-American workers arrive and realize the company was not holding their jobs any longer. They hoped the miners would relent and return to work, accepting whatever wage was offered. Similar tactics were used by a Pana coal company. The coal companies would lie to the African-American workers by telling them the miners had gone to war or quit, rather than explain the situation with the ongoing strike.

The Pana coal company was first in recruiting African-Americans to their mines. The men were sent on train to Pana in September 1898 and crossed the picket line. The unionized miners were furious that they had been replaced. The mine became an increasingly unruly place with fights breaking out between the strike breakers and those union miners. The area became so unsettled that Governor Tanner ordered state militia troops to standby in Pana in case anything got out of control.

The miners in Virden were dead-set against allowing anyone to take their jobs. They vowed that what happened in Pana would never happen at their mine. The miners assembled hundreds of workers from surrounding mines to line the railroad tracks at Virden and stop any strike breakers from stepping foot in the mine. The group of men appeared more like an armed camp, ready to attack, than it did a picket line. In spite of this, the men agreed to avoid violence and try to simply persuade the African-American workers to leave.

The first train showed up in late September 1898. Before stepping off the train, the Alabama workers were informed that they were entering a mine strike and upon seeing the large crowd gathered at the mine, they decided to keep moving down the tracks. The train then made its way to Springfield where it was met by the United Mine Workers President John Hunter. The

AFRICAN AMERICANS FROM ALABAMA ARRIVING IN ILLINOIS

men informed Mr. Hunter that they were deceived and had no idea a strike was the reason for the job openings. The men stated they wanted nothing to do with the strike and wished the miners all the luck in getting the wages they deserved. The train then left again, and the Alabama workers returned home.

On October 12, 1898, another train filled with unaware Alabama workers and their families was in route to Virden. Before arriving at the destination, the train stopped in East. St. Louis, where armed detectives from Thiel Detective Services boarded the train. The detectives were sent to protect the strike breakers and the coal company's interest. It was clear officials knew the situation could be dangerous but still they allowed the train to proceed to Virden.

As the train passed area stations, word began to travel to Virden that the strike breakers were on their way. When the train pulled into town, those on board saw the station swarming with people. It is estimated that over 1,500 miners from Virden and the surrounding communities were present. The miners were insistent that nobody would be getting off the train and the detectives refused to back down to the mob that awaited them. As the miners began to approach the train, the detectives fired their weapons into the crowd of miners. The passengers of the train fell to the floor and covered

An illustrated depiction of the Virden Massacre as the train pulled into town

themselves as best they could to avoid injury. They had no idea what was happening. All they knew was that their lives, and the lives of their families, were now in danger.

After approximately 20 minutes of gunfire and violence, the train left Virden and headed to Springfield with the African-American workers, their families, and the detectives still on board. When they arrived in Springfield, President Hunter tried to board the train, as he had previously, in an effort to explain what was going on, but the detectives refused to let him on board and he was beaten until he agreed to leave. Unfortunately for the others on board, they were left on the train for days while debated raged about what they should do. Either way, the Chicago-Virden Coal Company who recruited them refused to help. Should they try to go back to Virden and risk assault? Should they go to Pana and become strikebreakers there? If they wanted to go back home, how would they get there? Some did go to Pana and work in the mine, some went to St. Louis, and others returned home empty-handed with some help from the mine union.

Back in Virden, the miners were busy caring for the injured and tending to the dead. Blood covered the streets and local homes were turned into makeshift hospitals and morgues. It is believed that over 500 shots were fired that day. Eleven men died and over 35 were wounded.

Those who perished were:

D. N. KILEY, *Chicago & Alton detective.*
JOE GUILTEY, *Mount Olive.*
ELLIS SMITH, *Mount Olive.*
ED WALSH, *Springfield.*
EARNEST CAMERON, *Mount Olive.*
BERT SMITH, *Mount Olive.*
DAN BRENNEMAN, *Girard.*
W. W. CARROLL, *deputy sheriff.*
A. W. MORGAN, *stockade guard, Chicago.*
W. CLARKSON, *detective, Chicago.*
THOMAS PRESTON. *stockade guard, Chicago.*

Governor Tanner was blamed for causing the violence by allowing the trains of strike breakers to enter town, as well as poor management of police and officials. It was also revealed that the governor was telegrammed about the assembling miners and potential riot but chose not to send troops or aid to Virden.

More mine violence occurred in April and June the following year in Pana, where several others were killed and wounded over clashes between the union and strike breakers. The miners and coal companies eventually reached a resolution but for many, the end to the violence came too late.

MOTHER JONES

The Virden Massacre is remembered every year on October 12. The United Mine Workers built a cemetery in the small Macoupin County town of Mt. Olive, which has acted as a place of remembrance for the Virden tragedy, as well as for other mining disasters. Mother Jones, also known as Mary Harris Jones, is buried in the cemetery. Mother Jones is remembered as an activist who became known as "the most dangerous woman in America." She worked tirelessly with the United Mine Workers to help miners unionize and also worked to enforce child labor laws. She was a fierce lady who was respected by many of the local miners. Mother Jones passed away on November 30, 1930 at the age of 93. A monument in Mt. Olive stands in her honor.

Despite tragedies such as those in Virden, the coal industry continued to grow and by the early twentieth century, it was nearly impossible not to have at least one member of your family employed as a miner. In 1917, news broke that the Carlinville coal company had been sold to the Standard Oil Company of Indiana. The company bought 500 acres from Herman Schoper, a few miles outside of town, in order to expand the mine, which would fuel the Standard Oil refinery. The good news was that Standard Oil would be bringing over 1,500 new jobs to the area. The bad news was that miners were hard to find. The country was deeply invested in World War I and workers were few and far between, especially in a town that only had a population of a few thousand.

Standard Oil came up with an ingenious way to attract miners to Carlinville. They would offer them a place to call home. Starting in 1918, Standard Oil of Indiana placed a $1 million order with Sears, Roebuck and Company for 190 of their Sears Catalog Homes. These homes were a "build by numbers" type of operation where the homes arrived ready to assemble in a quick manner. There were 156 of the homes placed in Carlinville, 12 on the former Schoper property, and 24 in Wood River, where Standard Oil had a similar operation. The homes in Carlinville occupied approximately nine blocks in an area that was dubbed the "Standard Addition."

Today, Carlinville has the second largest collection of Sears Homes in the United States. The homes became so popular in town that the company even named one model the "Carlin," in honor of Carlinville.

The homes were offered at a reduced price with a generous mortgage payment plan to miners who would sign on at the mine. The offer attracted men with families to Carlinville and quickly increased the city's population and coal production. At the peak of mining, the Schoper mine was the largest in Illinois and produced roughly 4,000 tons of coal each day with over 600 men working in the mine. Another Carlinville mine was employing almost 500 people and producing over 2,000 tons daily.

Unfortunately, the good times didn't last. In 1925 Standard Oil closed the mines after deciding it was cheaper to purchase coal from non-union mines in Kentucky.

The miners who came to Carlinville in hopes of a better life for their family were now unemployed and most were unable to afford living in the Sears Homes. Foreclosure on the properties followed and the Standard Addition area of town was virtually abandoned. The Carlinville mines were

THE SEARS CATALOGUE HOMES IN THE PROCESS OF CONSTRUCTION

eventually re-opened by other corporations but never again brought the same hope and promise to the community that Standard Oil once did.

Besides being reliant on the employment of large companies that are only worried about making a profit, mining was also incredibly dangerous. Mining deaths were an tragically common headline in local newspapers.

One of Carlinville's most shocking mining accidents was relayed to me by my friend, Jennifer Reid Baugher, who discovered the story while researching some family history. On September 8, 1906, Joseph Hoelting and his son, Joseph, Jr., were working in a local mine. One of the coal cars came off the track and Joseph, Sr. instructed his son to go help the other men with the coal car and while he continued working. Out of nowhere, a large piece of coal fell from the ceiling of the mine, crushing Joseph, Sr. His son came back to find his father's lifeless body buried beneath the rubble. His death left five children fatherless and his pregnant wife a widow. Joseph, Jr. returned to work in the very mine where his father perished, working hard to support his mother and siblings. At the time of the accident, he was only 17-years-old. He continued to work in the mine until June 2, 1913, when, just like his father, he was killed by falling coal.

Other mining tragedies included the death of Joseph Begando in September 1942. He was killed instantly while working in the old Schoper mine. He was about 300 feet below the surface, near the entrance of the mine.

The Hoelting family is pictured above. Joseph Hoelting's wife Anna Maria was pregnant with their youngest son, August (pictured on his mother's lap) when her husband died. A 1900s version of Photoshop was used to insert her deceased husband, Joseph Sr., into the family photo.

He started loading a car with coal. The car was on what they called a "cage," which allowed the car full of coal to move throughout the mine. As he was loading the coal, the cage started to move, causing the car to roll backwards and coal to fall out. The falling coal pinned Joseph and he was killed.

Another notable tragedy occurred in January 1956 in the mining town of Gillespie, south of Carlinville. Battista Genta, a 64-year-old miner at Little Dog mine, was knocked down by 200 pounds of coal that fell from the ceiling. The impact knocked him forward onto a lever of one of the machines and it went straight through his head, just below his right eye. The gruesome accident was one the other miners would forever remember.

The risk of death and injury was always at the forefront of any smart miner's mind. He was wise to listen to any warnings of impending doom that might occur. Some of these warnings were given by canaries that were placed

GILLESPIE LITTLE DOG MINE

in cages in the mine. If the bird appeared sick or even died while in the mine, it was a sign that the air quality was dangerous and filled with carbon monoxide. It gave the miners a warning that it was time to leave the mine.

Other miners were said to receive warnings from something more unusual – the tommyknockers.

Tommyknockers are part of mining folklore and first made their presence known in the United States in Pennsylvania mines in the early 1800s by Celtic miners. Cornish miners believed the tommyknockers were the souls of those who crucified Jesus and were sent to work as slaves in the mines. Tommyknockers were said to be creatures about two-feet-high, similar in appearance to leprechauns or gnomes, but always wearing miner's clothing and even carrying mining tools. Some said the tommyknockers were really the souls of former miners who died and never left the mines while others argued that they'd never been human at all, but creatures that lurked underground.

Whatever their identity, it became known that miners would hear "knocks" on the mine wall right before a cave-in. They attributed this sound to the tommyknockers, who were warning them of impending danger. Most of the time the knocks would form a pattern and if a miner knocked back, they would usually get a response. Reports of unusual mist forming in mines just before a disaster, as well as unexplained balls of light were also attributed to tommyknockers

Some tommyknockers were good-natured and some were not. Some helped the miners, warning them of danger or even knocking in areas that were rich in coal as if they were working alongside them. Then there were tommyknockers who caused rock to fall in the mine, stole the lunches of the miners, or hid their tools. It was said that the way a tommyknocker responded to you depended on whether or not they liked you, plain and simple. Whatever you do, the old miners said, don't mock the tommyknocker. It was said that those who didn't believe, or made fun of the legend, would be plagued with bad luck and possibly even injury. The tales of the tommyknockers grew in popularity with the California Gold Rush. Miners out west were quick to blame the creatures for whatever fortune -- or misfortune -- they endured. Back home in Illinois, there were miners who shared in the tommyknocker beliefs and even those who didn't, didn't dare tempt fate by discounting the creatures.

My own family has a history in Macoupin County coal mining. Virtually every male in my father's generation, and those prior, was involved in coal mining. Both sides of my family, Italian and Scottish, immigrated to Illinois and sought out the mining industry to help them pursue their American dream. Many other families in the area have similar histories. The town of Gillespie even houses a coal museum and their high school mascot is the Miners.

Even though most of the mines in the area have since closed, there are some that remain and even those that don't, continue to make an impact. In July 2009, unprecedented mine subsidence struck a Benld Elementary school, roughly 15 miles south of Carlinville. A teacher noticed some hair-line cracks outside her classroom and by the next day the entire school had suffered considerable damage. Cracks in the building were inches wide, walls were crumbling, pipes were twisted, and the entire floor was buckled and bowed, dropping as much as two feet in some places. Benld was a mining town and the school was built over a former mining site. During construction, pillars were placed to prop up the school, but the mine had started to collapse, and the pillars were failing. The 78,000-square-foot, recently constructed school for 700 children was declared unsafe. The children were left without a school and the former mining town was left with a vacant building. Eventually, the children got a new elementary school. This time, though, it was placed in the nearby town of Gillespie and away from the sinking mine.

Disaster struck Benld again in April 2015 when mine subsidence occurred overnight. A police officer noticed bowing in the middle of the street and a quick drive around town showed additional mine subsidence damage in a total of about six blocks. Unfortunately for me, I was living in one of those six blocks at the time. The subsidence caused damage to numerous homes. Walls and foundations were cracked, garages were shifted, and concrete driveways were broken. Some even had their front steps pulled away from the house and they were unable to open doors in their homes because the entire structure had shifted. Over 70 homes in the area, mine included, were without power for several days as methane gas was detected in several homes. We were told that staying in the area was at our own risk due to possible methane explosions. I remember that for the next several days you could see the water in puddles outside bubbling, likely from the escaping mine gas. My sewer didn't work properly, and the drains gurgled eerily every time I tried to drain water. Eventually, my sewer line broke. You can imagine the cleanup wasn't pretty. I no longer live in Benld and I'm thankful, especially because the abandoned mine problem continues.

While all this was going on, I remember waking up one night to a loud noise. I found nothing out of place and went back to bed. I assume it was the sound of the earth shifting but what if it was something else?

I can't help but wonder if maybe it was a tommyknocker, or miner's ghost, warning of the dangers to come? Either way there is no doubt the mines continue to hold a mysterious danger that will forever affect the people of Macoupin County.

9. ALL ROADS LEAD TO BOOZE
ROUTE 66 AND MACOUPIN COUNTY'S GANGSTERS

Known as "America's Main Street" and the "Mother Road," Route 66 was one of the original highways in the U.S. Highway System. Established officially in November 1926, the highway became the most famous road in America. It originally ran from Chicago, Illinois, through Missouri, Kansas, Oklahoma, Texas, New Mexico, Arizona, and ended in Santa Monica, California. It spawned hit songs, television shows, books, and a nostalgic longing for America's good old days.

Route 66 served as the main road for those who migrated west, especially during the Dust Bowl era of the 1930s, and it created a living for the small towns along the route that became prosperous because of restaurants, motor lodges, and roadside attractions. These same people fought to keep Route 66 alive when it began to be replaced by the new interstate system.

Route 66 in Illinois originally passed through Carlinville and while it was diverted several times in the early 1930s, it left a permanent mark on the city. Carlinville was the first home of the Ariston Café, a Route 66 landmark. When it was opened by Pete Adam in 1924, it was a quiet place with two gas pumps out front. But when Route 66 came through Carlinville, Pete's business began to thrive. The Ariston soon became known as the "most up-to-date restaurant between Chicago and St. Louis."

In 1931, Route 66 was re-routed east to Litchfield and the Carlinville café went into a decline. Refusing to give up, Pete moved the Ariston to Litchfield and he did so well that he had to construct a new building in 1935. Vice

THE ARISTON CAFE IN ITS ORIGINAL LOCATION ON THE CARLINVILLE SQUARE

President Hubert Humphrey once ate at the restaurant, as did band leader Tommy Dorsey. It's still open today, serving over 100 customers at a time and looking pretty much just as it did in the 1930s.

Over the years, Route 66 was rerouted several times through Litchfield and each change made it necessary to move the front door of the restaurant to keep it facing the road. As fate would have it, with the last realignment, the restaurant entrance ended up at the original front location.

The 1926 layout of Route 66 follows the current Illinois 4 highway in Macoupin County. You can still see remnants of the old Route 66 alongside portions of the highway. Route 66 created a paved route from Chicago to St. Louis, with Macoupin County smack dab in the center.

Route 66 became known as a dangerous road. In fact, some called it "Bloody 66" or "Bloody Highway." The Route allowed cars to travel at higher speeds than ever before, whipping through small towns that weren't accustomed to fast-moving vehicles. Countless auto accidents and deaths occurred on the highway, one of which I have a very close connection with.

My great-grandmother Mary Rooney Brown worked odd jobs to help support her large family, which lived about 16 miles south of Carlinville near the small town of Mt. Clare, Illinois. One of her jobs was to tend to the laundry of a nearby neighbor. Early in the morning she would walk over to their home, crossing Route 66, to retrieve their clothes and bring them home to wash and dry. It was a cold morning on December 31, 1933, but Mary bundled up herself and her 11-year-old daughter, Agnes, so she could make the trip to the neighbor's home for laundry. It was early in the morning and the haze of winter days clouded the sky. Mother and daughter began to cross the highway, hand in hand, as they had so many times before. Without warning a truck appeared. The truck's speed was far too great to avoid. Mary Rooney quickly realized there was no time for both of them to make a dash to the other side to safety, so she grabbed her daughter and pushed her as hard as she could out of the way of the truck. Her daughter fell at the side of the road and Mary Rooney was struck and killed by the speeding vehicle. The truck continued on its way, never stopping to offer assistance. Agnes ran to get help, but her mother couldn't be saved. The danger of that "Bloody Highway" left my great-grandfather, Norman, a widower, and left his seven children without a mother, the youngest of which was three-year-old Robert, my grandfather.

MARY ROONEY BROWN

Despite the dangers, Route 66 enhanced travel ten-fold. It created an all-weather road that was easy to follow and easy to travel. I imagine that some of Route 66's biggest fans were some of Illinois' most notorious travelers. Prohibition existed between 1920 and 1933 and Route 66 gave those involved in bootlegging an easy way to transport alcohol between speakeasies.

THE CARLINVILLE CONNECTION

One of Carlinville's most prominent legends involves the famous route and one of America's most famous gangsters, Al Capone, also known as "Public Enemy Number One" and "Scarface." Alphonse Capone was born January 17, 1899, in Brooklyn. After moving to Chicago, he worked his way up to become the boss of the Chicago Outfit, controlling most of the crime and liquor in the city. Capone and his men became expert bootleggers and

ORTIC INN

operated scores of distilleries, breweries, gambling houses and brothels throughout Illinois. Some say he even spent some time in Macoupin County.

Right outside of Carlinville, on property now owned by Lake Williamson, there was an old barn located in the northeast corner. The barn is said to have been a Sears and Roebuck Cyclone model that was purchased by Chicago native, Louis Citro. In 1919, Louis moved to Carlinville and started a dairy farm on the property. Louis also built a building dubbed the Ortic Inn (his last named spelled backwards) which housed four bedrooms, a kitchen, bathroom, and more impressively a ballroom, bandstand, and sunroom used for illegal gambling.

Due to the illegal activities on the property and the Citro family's Chicago roots, those around Carlinville began to suspect that Citro was involved with the Chicago mob and even Al Capone himself. A man by the name of Frank Citro, also known as Frank "Frost" Foster, due to his icy expressions, was known to be a seasoned mafia member, and many assumed Louis Citro was linked to the mobster. Foster was a ruthless man who was responsible for several murders, including that – some claimed -- of *Chicago-Tribune* reporter, Jake Lingle.

Even though Louis showed no signs of the same vicious tendencies, it didn't stop the public from speculating about his reputation. Rumors started to swirl that Louis, through an association with Frank, supplied bootleg liquor to the Capone gang. Some even reported that Capone would keep one of his vehicles in the old barn on the Citro property for safe-keeping and to be used for travel when visiting downstate Illinois.

The truth is this is all speculation.

The connection between Louis Citro and Frank Citro isn't clear. In fact, about the only thing that can be verified is that they shared a last name.

Now don't get me wrong, Louis Citro was not innocent, and he may very well have been involved in some sort of mob-related activity. In fact, I believe he most likely was. It was widely-known that Louis kept a large supply of liquor in his barn. Prohibition made possession of alcohol illegal and by 1924, it wasn't just the locals who knew about Louis's stash. In August 1924, the Citro property was raided by authorities. It didn't take them long to find the liquor that had been hidden in the barn. Citro was arrested, along with several other workers at the Ortic Inn. The men were arraigned on charges of violating the federal prohibition laws. Initially, Louis plead not guilty. He stated the liquor was for personal consumption and not for sale, hoping to lessen the charges against him. Along with his attorney, he argued the charges should be dropped completely due to illegal search and seizure of his property.

By March 1925, it appeared as though the case was going to trial. Louis's attorney realized there would be little sympathy for a wealthy land owner who had an affinity for booze. He wisely decided to negotiate a plea deal for his client. Louis and three of his employees pled guilty to lesser charges. Louis was fined $1,500 for alcohol possession, and the three others -- Frank Depasquaic, Darrel Morrison, and Joe Cusiman -- were fined $500 and given nine months in jail on charges of possession, public nuisance, and sale of liquor. It goes to show you that those who can afford to hire a competent attorney are more likely to avoid jail time.

After the raid, the Ortic Inn was closed down and the Citro family returned to Chicago. The "farm" became an actual working farm and managers were hired to operate things. In the winter of 1936, they started a new venture, cutting and storing ice on the property, which they would sell for use in the summer months.

The following year the Citro family would again be in the local newspapers. The caretaker of the property, Dan Marshall, along with his wife, went missing. Authorities believed Marshall had abandoned the farm, which led to the death of seven hogs, one cow, and 30 chickens, as well as the potential starvation of countless other animals. A neighboring farmer, Roy Smith, noticed he had not seen Marshall for about a week and became concerned. When he arrived on the Citro property, he was shocked to find the place abandoned. An investigation determined that the Marshalls left on their own accord. They took nine head of cattle and some hogs with them when they went. In East St. Louis, they used the fake name of Dave Jones to sell the livestock for cash. The reason for their sudden departure remains a mystery and the Marshalls were never heard from again.

The Citros eventually found a new caretaker and continued the farming business. In 1946, the Stetter family leased out the old Ortic Inn and renamed it the Artic Inn. The Artic Inn served as the family's home, as well as a nightclub that operated from 1946 to 1950. In 1959, the Citro family sold the farmland to a man named Randall Loveless, who in turn sold it to the Illinois

Assemblies of God organization, which now runs Lake Williamson Christian Center on the property.

There is no solid evidence to say that Al Capone ever visited the Ortic Inn, let alone used the barn as a garage. However, I do feel it's probable that Louis Citro was involved in the distribution of alcohol during the years of prohibition. I can't think of any other reason why he would have hundreds of illegal liquor stashed on his property. Even the most severe alcoholic wouldn't be able to drink a barn full of booze.

In the early 2000s, Lake Williamson volunteers cleared out the old barn and found several longneck liquor bottles hidden away in the walls. No surprise there. Louis Citro likely operated a speakeasy and was paid off to store liquor on his property until it could be transported to other locations – locations like a popular nightspot that was just up the road in Benld.

BOOTLEGGERS OF BENLD

Macoupin County was home to other illicit establishments, with one community standing out ahead of all the others when it came to liquor and vice. The town of Benld was founded in 1903. It was organized and named by Ben L. Dorsey – literally. Legend has it that the sign leading into town was once damaged by a storm, leaving only part of the name behind: "Ben L. D." The shorter name was apparently easier to remember.

Dorsey sold 40,000 acres of coal and mining rights to the Superior Coal Company, cementing the town's reputation for mining. Immigrants from all over, especially Italy, came to Benld in search of jobs, including my father's family.

The town grew and by the early 1920s, it was estimated that over 3,300 people called Benld home. Grocery stores, barbershops, lumber yards, and soda factories made Benld a successful town. By the start of prohibition, they also had nearly 40 taverns. That seems like a lot of taverns for such a small town, but the miners liked to drink, and the tavern owners liked taking their money. You can see how Prohibition created both a problem and an opportunity for those in Benld.

When American alcohol distributers were forced out of business by Prohibition, entrepreneurs in Benld decided to manufacture it themselves. I like to think that those from Benld were just "go getters," who found a solution to a problem. Unfortunately, that solution was highly illegal. On the edge of Benld, in a wooded area, the "No. 5 mine" opened. This mine was slightly different than those which sought coal -- this one produced alcohol. The "No. 5 mine" was a distillery with three 50-foot smokestacks and around-the-clock security. The distillery was a success and produced hundreds of

DOWNTOWN IN WHAT WAS ONCE THE THRIVING TOWN OF BENLD

gallons of whiskey each week. While this was the most advanced distillery in the area, it was not the only one. Numerous others were operated throughout Benld. The owners of the illegal stills were mostly kept under wraps, although that didn't stop people in town from talking. If the still was large enough it was almost guaranteed that organized crime was involved. Sure, some in town had a still for personal use, or for use in their local tavern, but if the operation was producing hundreds of gallons of liquor, like the "No. 5 Mine," it was most certainly being transported to other parts of the state. That's where the mob came in.

The town is somewhat split on whether or not mob boss Al Capone was involved in Benld distilleries. Some point to the fact that there is no documented evidence that Al Capone or his gang ever came to Benld, let alone operated an illegal distillery. To that I have to respond, if Al Capone *did* operate out of Benld, he wouldn't want you to know and would do whatever he could to make sure you didn't.

It's worth noting that Benld is a "Little Italy" of sorts. The town is rooted in Italian immigrants. The Italian flag is still hung outside the homes of many in town and they still celebrate the town's Italian American Days each year. Having come from an Italian family that lived in Benld, I can tell you that those in the area can, and will, keep a secret. It's only in more recent years that "old timers" of Benld have come forward with their memories of the gangsters that hung out in town.

My grandmother, who we always referred to as Nonni, as well as my great-grandmother, Rena Scopel Rosa (Nona), would share memories of experiences and stories heard during the Prohibition days. My great-grandmother was born in 1912 and grew up in Benld. She spent most of her free time playing outside and along the streets of the downtown area. She could remember Capone's gang coming into town to check on their businesses. Referred to sometimes as "Uncle Al's gang," the mobsters fascinated the area children. They would pull into town with their fancy cars, gorgeous suits, and a no-nonsense attitude that demanded attention. Even though their presence was often intimidating, they always treated the children in Benld kindly, even throwing them a coin or two, sometimes upwards to a half-dollar! I still have some of what Nonni called her "gangster coins."

In the mid-1930s my grandfather, Robert Brown, had an uneasy encounter with the area mobsters. He was traveling with his family in their car to Gillespie, coming from Mt. Clare. Suddenly, the car hit some black ice and slid, causing the car to end horizontal across the road, blocking the other lane. The ice made it impossible for the car to gain traction and it became stuck. My grandfather's cousin, Bill, got out of the car and tried to give it a shove to get it moving, but he kept sliding on the ice. A few moments later, a black touring car came up behind their vehicle. It came to a stop, unable to pass due to the peculiar position of the other vehicle. My grandfather vividly recalls seeing a group of gangsters emerge from the car with their tommy guns ready for action. Cousin Bill stood there looking at the gangsters, and calmly lit his cigar. The gangsters looked at one another and realized that the car blocking the road wasn't a rival gang setting a roadblock, it was a family stuck on some ice. A few of the gangsters made their way over to the family vehicle. My grandfather remembers seeing one of the gangsters approach the car window near where he was sitting. He thought to himself, "this is it, they're going to shoot us." Instead, without saying a word, the gangsters picked up the rear end of the vehicle and moved it to the side of the road. Then they returned to their car and took off down the road.

Another popular family story comes from my father. My father grew up in the Benld area and always knew about the scandalous history of the little town. His large Italian family from Benld gave him the opportunity to learn firsthand the stories of Prohibition and gangsters. A child of the late 1950s and early 60s, he often spent his free time playing outside or walking around town and visiting with neighbors. One of the neighbors he would often visit was an old gangster who went by the name "Mugsy." Even though Mugsy was now an elderly man, the stories of his youth reflected a once energetic and no-nonsense mobster. Mugsy would often tell of his wild days of bootlegging and robbing, which eventually landed him in prison. As time passed, Mugsy began to trust my father and pay him for odd jobs. My dad would wash his car, get his groceries, and even deliver items to others in the neighborhood on behalf of the former gangster. He became known as a delivery and errand boy of sorts and he was happy to do it. Mugsy always had cash on hand to pay him and for a young boy the adventure and thrill of helping the old mobster was payment enough.

ONE OF THE RUMORED PROHIBITION "WHORE HOUSES" ON OLD ROUTE 66 IN BENLD

Years ago, I asked my Nonni why everyone called my dad "Sonny" instead of his given name "George." She replied, "The old gangsters in town always used to call him "sonny boy" and it stuck."

As child I spent a lot of time in Benld with my father's family. Even though I was very young, I recall some of those old gangsters and Benld natives chatting with my Nonni on the porch. They always referred to me as "Sonny's girl" and would often pat me on the head and hand me some cash or stick it in my shoe. I never understood what that meant but I never turned down the free money. My stories are just a few of many. Numerous other families report similar memories and family tales of the gangsters in Benld, which convinces me even further that gangsters were present in Macoupin County.

It wasn't just the distilleries that brought mobsters to the area, it was the brothels. Mobsters including Al Capone not only ran bootlegging operations, but they ran brothels as well. In fact, brothels were the only business in town that even came close to outnumbering the taverns. There should have been a welcome sign that read, "You have entered Benld, come for the brothel, stay for the booze."

To give you a glimpse into the amount of liquor available in Benld, I will refer to a raid that took place in July 1920. When prohibition officers from East St. Louis strolled into town, they found six stills, 800 gallons of whiskey, and 800 gallons of raisin mash, leading to the arrest of 16 saloon owners. The next month a fire destroyed the Benld jail. The *Ashton Gazette* newspaper reported the jail had "enough liquors and wines to stock a small saloon." Even the jail was stocked full of booze!

While the gangsters were blamed for a lot of the debauchery in Benld, the police weren't always so innocent either. In November 1927, local police officer Charles Purdy and James Leone, a coal dealer, were out drinking in Benld. As they walked down a sidewalk, James playfully told the officer, "if you're drunk you should go find a place to sit down," and pushed him off the sidewalk. Officer Purdy retaliated and punched James Leone in the jaw, causing him to fall and hit his head. The man died instantly, and the officer was charged with murder.

Benld Police Chief Bolini was often ridiculed by other police agencies for his refusal to arrest bootleggers. He was quoted as saying, "The federal authorities started it. Let them finish it." It's easy to see why the lawless citizens of Benld wanted that man appointed as sheriff.

In 1929, the Capone gang murdered seven members of the rival North Side Gang (Moran Gang) in Chicago. The event would become known as the St. Valentine's day Massacre. That same year Macoupin County experienced its own holiday massacre. On March 31, 1929, Easter Sunday, Frank "Curly" Hines and his brother-in-law, Smith Tucker, were driving into Wilsonville, a small town a few miles from Benld. A big blue sedan drove up behind their vehicle and the men inside began yelling at Frank and Smith to exit their vehicle. Smith stopped the car and Frank got out and started walking towards the sedan. The men in the sedan then pulled out machine guns and started firing at Frank Hines. His body was riddled with bullets before falling to the ground. With no time to escape, Smith trapped in the driver's seat of his car. The men turned their guns in his direction and filled the car full of holes. They jumped back in their sedan and sped away. The massacre was witnessed by a group of young boys who were playing outside at the time, but they refused to give the police much information.

The motive for the murders was thought to be mob related. Frank "Curly" Hines was involved with bootleggers and mobsters in both Chicago and Detroit. In fact, he was a current suspect in a bank robbery in Davenport, Iowa, and had previously robbed a jewelry store in Springfield, Illinois, and stolen a car in Alton. He was also a known friend of Byron Bolton, a Chicago gangster and Capone affiliate who grew up on a farm near the Macoupin County town of Virden. Byron would later be known as a snitch who gave a confession to federal agents, pinpointing the Capone gang as the ones responsible for the St. Valentine's day Massacre.

Roughly a year and a half prior, in December 1927, Frank had been entrusted with a truck filled with over $15,000 in liquor. When he arrived in Chicago to deliver the liquor, he said he had been hijacked and the liquor was stolen. Later, word got out that liquor resembling the type and quantity entrusted to Frank was being sold on the street. It was assumed that Frank had schemed his own crew and sold the liquor himself.

Authorities believed the shooting was retaliation for Frank's double crossing and carelessness and fear about his recent arrests. It's that possible Frank's bosses were worried he would spill information about the bootlegging operation when faced with his theft charges. Killing Frank might have been a failsafe. As far as Smith Tucker was concerned, he was a tragic casualty. The identity of the mobsters who carried out the murders was never learned, although many believe they were likely tied to the Capone gang. Shortly after the massacre, locals began reporting that Capone's men were in Macoupin County, perhaps to make sure the job was done. Local newspapers also reported that members of the Capone gang were seen in Springfield soon after the shooting. Frank's friendship with Byron Bolton also supports the idea that Frank may very well have been affiliated with Capone.

There was no doubt Benld lived up to its wild reputation. Even if Al Capone himself wasn't frequenting Benld, recorded history shows that someone was pulling the strings to keep the liquor flowing in town. This person was also powerful enough to get rid of any problems that might arise.

On December 24, 1924, Benld resident Dominic Tarro opened the Coliseum Ballroom in town. The building was spectacular and could hold up to 800 dancers. Even more astounding was the ballroom's price tag, costing Dominic $50,000 which would be over $700,000 today! It was perplexing how Dominic, who had previously worked as a butcher and rate clerk, could afford to invest such an amazing amount of money. Well, there were some theories about how Dominic was able to open the ballroom. Rumors around town reported Dominic was financed by gangsters who wanted to use the ballroom as a hideout and a stop for liquor runners between Chicago and St. Louis. While you can't always believe what you hear, this time the rumors seemed to be true.

In January 1930, Dominic Tarro was indicted on federal charges of Prohibition violation and conspiracy. Others indicted included the Corn Products Refining Company, the Fleischmann Yeast Company, and 17

COLISEUM BALLROOM

bootleggers. The government alleged that the Corn Products Company shipped more than 200 carloads of corn sugar from its refineries, which were then taken to distilleries in and around Benld. The government accused the Fleischmann Yeast company of the same, except supplying yeast instead of sugar. Dominic was said to be the facilitator between the companies, bootleggers, and mobsters, as well as the manager of the "No. 5 Mine" in Benld. However, there was one person who believed Dominic was innocent -- his wife, Marie. She was adamant that her husband was just a simple sugar dealer in Benld.

Dominic arranged bail and was able to return home while awaiting trial, although he was likely better off staying in prison. On January 29, 1930, he arranged to drive to Springfield to meet with his lawyer, but fate had other plans. Dominic disappeared. A few days later, police found Dominic's car marked by bullet holes and burned along Route 43, five miles from Mason City. An empty gas can, thought to fuel the fire was found nearby. There were two schools of thought on Dominic's disappearance -- he either staged his disappearance to avoid criminal charges and the mob or he was kidnapped. The truth wouldn't be known until several months later.

On May 2, 1930, the naked body of a man was found among some driftwood near a bridge in the Sangamon river. His arms and feet were bound together with wire and another wire was tied around the neck to pull the head down to the feet. The man had been badly beaten before he was executed and tossed in the river. Even though the body was in the advanced stages of decomposition, an appendicitis scar led authorities to the dead man's identity.

It was Dominic Tarro.

Some believed Dominic was killed due to fears that he would become an informant in exchange for immunity. Others reported Dominic was lured to meet his associates under the assumption that he was going to collect money he was owed. Clues into who was responsible for Dominic's death arrived by mail shortly after his body was found. Rocco Richichi from Collinsville was serving a federal sentence in the Springfield prison for charges related to bootlegging. Rocco would occasionally do business with Dominic, having him arrange supplies for his still. When he was sent to prison, his associates agreed to pay Rocco's wife $5 per day as a way to make sure that Rocco would keep his mouth shut while in jail. After a time, his associates decided to cut his wife's hush money to $50 a month, which was $100 less per month than originally agreed. Rocco became furious and revealed information to authorities that resulted in several arrests. Obviously, his associates didn't appreciate him coming forward and they began to send him threatening letters. The authorities tried to trace the letters, believing this would lead them to Dominic's killers, but the clues led nowhere.

There was a lot of speculation about who was really running the show in Benld. Some believed it was mobsters from St. Louis. Others still believed it was the Chicago mob, tied to Capone. Another contender was Springfield mob boss Frank Zito.

Frank had a history with Benld. In 1915, Frank stabbed a Benld miner and robbed him of $10. The miner died but Frank never faced any consequences. The year prior, Frank's brother, Sam, tried to extort money from an Italian businessman in Benld. Sam sent a letter to the man threatening his life if he was not paid what he was seeking. The threatening letter sounds awfully familiar to the one Rocco Richichi received in prison which adds to the speculation the Zitos were involved in Dominic's murder. Frank Zito was also included in the federal indictment with Dominic Tarro. Frank, under the cover of his grocery business, was accused of distributing sugar to the local distilleries. It was well known that Frank blamed Dominic for the legal trouble and he most certainly wasn't shy when it came to violence. It is also coincidental that Dominic went missing in Springfield, which is where the Zito gang was located. It seems Frank Zito and his gang had means, motive, and opportunity. Whoever it was, they were never prosecuted. For the most part, the others involved in the indictment got off easy. Since Dominic was

FRANK ZITO

really the only person who knew the bulk of the incriminating information, the charges against the other plaintiffs were less than the federal government originally hoped, and most were only fined and received little to no jail time.

In the last three years of Dominic's life, he made a total of $238,000, which is over $3 million today. Hard to believe that a simple sugar salesman and a ballroom owner was a millionaire three times over, isn't it? I think we all can agree that Dominic Tarro was one of the most successful bootleggers in Macoupin County. Unfortunately for him, that success cost him his life.

Towards the end of Dominic's run as the Macoupin County bootlegger middle man, distilleries were becoming increasing difficult to conceal. Even the infamous "No. 5 Mine" was raided in March of 1928. Federal officials found two 50,000-gallon vats and 1,000 gallons of alcohol ready for transport. The distillery was valued at around $175,000 (over $2.5 million today). Agents quickly destroyed the still, gathered the engine and boilers to sell for junk metal, and using dynamite to destroy the rest. Another Benld still was raided a few months later, producing 175 gallons of ready-to-ship alcohol. Raids on Macoupin County distilleries continued until the end of prohibition in 1933.

The Tarro legacy lived on in the Coliseum Ballroom, which Marie Tarro ran after his husband's death. The couple's daughter, Joyce, would later take over the operation in 1955. The list of performers at the coliseum is impressive. Stars such as Tommy Dorsey, Lawrence Welk, and Duke Ellington performed in the coliseum's early years. Chuck Berry, Chubby Checker, Ray Charles, The Everly Brothers, and Ike and Tina Turner packed the building in later years. A *State Journal Register* article reported Elvis Presley had booked a show in the 1950s but ended up canceling. It also spoke of how Joyce Tarro turned down booking the Beatles in 1964 because she wasn't convinced anyone would pay to hear them. You can't win them all, I suppose.

The Coliseum became a popular spot for entertainment and hosted not only talented musicians but also local dances, parties, weddings, and even roller skating. Joyce worked hard to ensure the success of the Coliseum and was known to be a tough, yet fair, business woman. She didn't fool around, and she regularly reminded anyone who threatened trouble at the Coliseum that she carried a gun and wasn't afraid to use it. Even though she would often be the last one to leave the building late at night, she never felt unsafe. She even had the habit of carrying the ballroom's receipts home with her without a second thought about potential danger.

A Valentine's Day celebration was held at the Coliseum Ballroom on February 16, 1976. Those in attendance recalled the ballroom being packed with patrons and the five bartenders constantly busy serving drinks. The party brought Joyce a nice profit. At the end of the night, as she had done countless times before, Joyce packed up the cash from the ballroom and returned home. As she entered her house at around 2:30 a.m., she was confronted by two intruders, a man and a woman. They shot Joyce six times and she fell to the ground. The feisty woman returned fire but died shortly after. The thieves stole the $3,300 that Joyce was carrying, quickly climbed in a waiting car, and drove away.

All together there were four people involved in the robbery and murder. Jerry Tate Baker of Decatur acted as the lookout and get-away driver, while Rob King of Decatur and Mary Kay Hughes Conner of Gillespie waited inside the home for Joyce to arrive. After the murder, another man from Decatur drove King and Conner out west as they tried to evade the police. Despite their attempts to avoid capture, the couple was arrested only a few days later in Grand Junction, Colorado. Their car had broken down and authorities got word of their location. They were able to apprehend them at a nearby bus station. The driver of the vehicle was offered immunity in exchange for his testimony.

Jerry Baker also arranged a deal with the prosecution in exchange for information and testimony and he was sentenced to two to six years for robbery. The murder trial against King and Conner lasted seven days. After about two and a half hours, the jury returned a verdict of guilty. The killers each received 50-150 years for murder, 25-75 years for armed robbery, plus 10 years for theft.

In her will, Joyce left the Coliseum to a friend and former Benld resident, Bonnie Anderson. The Coliseum did re-open under the management of Joyce's cousin, Bud Tarro, but it didn't last. The Coliseum was then leased to locals Patty Ferraro and Hiram Franzoi. Efforts were made to keep the ballroom alive, but it just wasn't the same without Joyce. As the years passed, a slew of people tried to revive the Coliseum to its former glory but it never really panned out.

When the Coliseum Ballroom opened as an antique mall in the 1990s, people began to notice that something strange was occurring in the old building. During its early days as an antique mall, a woman with short dark hair would often be spotted in the upstairs area. She would be there one second and disappear the next, with no explanation. People began to whisper that the historic ballroom was haunted.

Another ghostly apparition of a man was also reported. The man was said to appear on a back staircase that was inaccessible to the public and vanish. Strange mists were also reported in the building, as well as cold spots and chilled breezes that occurred even on the hottest of summer days.

As I sit here writing about the Coliseum Ballroom, I've been experiencing my own version of the unexplained. While typing I began to hear big band music. I looked around and noticed the television was off and my laptop and iPad didn't have any websites pulled up where music should be playing. I checked my phone and it was quiet. A few more seconds passed, and the music stopped. I looked around, searching for someone to give me an explanation, but I was all alone. I'm sure there is a logical explanation for the music, but it did get me thinking about all the secrets and mysteries of the ballroom. Sadly, any further investigation into the hauntings of the building will never happen.

The antique mall operated for several years but eventually moved to another location off the interstate. Others inhabited the ballroom after that, operating an antique mall and then as a venue for live music, returning to the building's musical roots.

On July 31, 2011, the coliseum offered a free concert featuring the local band, Shadow of a Doubt. At around 9:00 p.m., a fire broke out in the building. By the time fire crews arrived, the building was engulfed in flames. Approximately 30 people were inside at the time. The fire was intense and quickly consumed the roof, raining burning tiles down on those inside. More than 15 fire departments worked tirelessly to fight the fire, but the building could not be saved. The only thing that would remain was the iconic front of the building, as well as its classic neon sign. The charred remnants of the once glorious building were eventually bulldozed.

The lot now sits empty, and the Coliseum acts as its own type of ghost, void of the walls that built it, but still felt by those who pass its location along the former Route 66.

10. MACOUPIN'S MILLION DOLLAR MYSTERY
HISTORY AND HAUNTINGS OF THE MACOUPIN COUNTY COURTHOUSE

There is one building in Macoupin County that surpasses all the rest when it comes to its superb construction, elaborate design, and exquisite beauty. It also takes the prize for the most scandal, mysteries, and spirits. It sits a short walk off the Carlinville square and greets visitors with the sight of its impressive dome as they enter town. The Macoupin County Courthouse, also known as the "Million Dollar Courthouse," proves to be one of the most fascinating locations you can still visit in the area. It boasts over 150 years of history, much of which is still present within its limestone walls.

The story of the Million Dollar Courthouse starts at the end of the Civil War. At the time, the county was still using the courthouse that was located on the town square. That courthouse had become crowded and outdated, forcing many county offices, such as the assessor and treasurer, to be located in an entirely different building. Those who worked in the courthouse were becoming increasingly tired of the cramped quarters. One of those frustrated courthouse workers was county Judge Thaddeus Loomis.

In 1863, Judge Loomis, who was also given authority regarding the county's finances, arranged the purchase of eight lots for $1,300 in the location where the Million Dollar Courthouse currently sits. For several years, county officials debated whether or not the county should construct a new courthouse. Sure, the current courthouse was a bit small, but it carried a lot of pride and hosted Carlinville friend Abraham Lincoln when he was a lawyer. Many in town felt a personal connection with the building and weren't ready to give it up.

Two years later, Judge Loomis was running for re-election. It was clear that a vote for Loomis was a vote for a new courthouse. By this time, the county was more receptive to investing the time and money into a bigger and better courthouse. Some say it was the talk about splitting Macoupin County into two separate counties that motivated Carlinville locals to support the new courthouse. They believed a new courthouse which would ensure Carlinville kept the county seat. Whatever their reasons, the citizens voted for Judge Loomis and made plans for a new courthouse.

In February 1867, at the request of county commissioners, the state authorized the county to borrow $50,000 (over $800,000 today) as well as issue bonds and levy taxes to pay for the new courthouse. A 50-cent levy was placed on every $100 worth of property and while nobody likes a tax increase, it was understood by most that this investment would be well worth it when they had a brand-new courthouse.

The following month, the county commissioners appointed Alexander Dubois (associate of the Chestnut and Dubois bank), George Holliday (the county clerk), Isham J. Peebles (county judge), and already outspoken courthouse supporter, Judge Loomis, as the courthouse commissioners, also known as the Courthouse Committee. The banking firm of Chestnut and Dubois was appointed as the financial institution for the new construction and Judge Loomis was selected as the financial agent who possessed full authority to access funds.

Citizens of the county assumed the new courthouse would be built on the square, the same location as the other two previous courthouses. However, it was soon evident the new courthouse's features would be much too grand to fit on the Carlinville square. Architect Elijah E. Meyers from Springfield won the construction contract. He was an accomplished architect who would later go on to design countless other courthouses, capital buildings, and city halls.

The courthouse committee spent $24,800, almost half the initial budget, for 16 blocks to the east of the square, near the Carlinville River, which today is underground. The land was mostly vacant, although a few houses did exist and were promptly bought and torn down to make room for the Macoupin County jewel.

Concern among the citizens began to grow with the purchase of the land. A meeting was arranged at the old courthouse to address the worries about the location of the courthouse and the expenses that had already taken place. Those in attendance heard speeches from both sides of the fence and before the night was over it was agreed that the new budget would be raised up to $150,000 but the courthouse would remain located on the square. Despite the understood agreement, the Courthouse Committee didn't follow through with the desire to keep the courthouse on the Carlinville square, although they were happy to expand the budget. Building would continue with architect Myers choosing a Renaissance Revival Style for the new building.

ELIJAH E. MYERS

Additional meetings were organized to discuss the citizens' outrage over the apparent disregard the Courthouse Committee had about their wishes. Area towns adopted proclamations against the committee officials and formed their own "anti-courthouse" committees. I.M. Metcalf, a chairman in Carlinville, stated, the county court has: "disregarded the almost unanimous and oft-repeated protest of the people of this count; that it has utterly disregarded the best interests of the people and has imposed a debt that the present generation may not hope to be able to cancel." He publicly called the county out on "shameful violations" and "tyranny," which were sentiments shared by many in the area.

Ignoring the pleas of citizens, the county proceeded with the construction of the new courthouse. The commissioners made an arrangement with the Chicago and Alton Railroad to form a spur track that would allow flatcars to be loaded with materials and pulled by oxen to the property. The track became known as "Ox Railroad" and it remained in place until November of 1869. The county also began hiring workers for the construction project. They directed their advertising at ex-slaves who were in need of work after the Civil War. Many of those who came to Carlinville to work on the courthouse project would later become Macoupin County citizens.

The groundbreaking ceremony took place in July of 1867. Mountains of limestone, brick, an iron arrived daily via the Ox Railroad. A 10-foot-high fence was quickly built to keep out bystanders and curious eyes, which only fueled the fire of the disgruntled county citizens. What were they building in

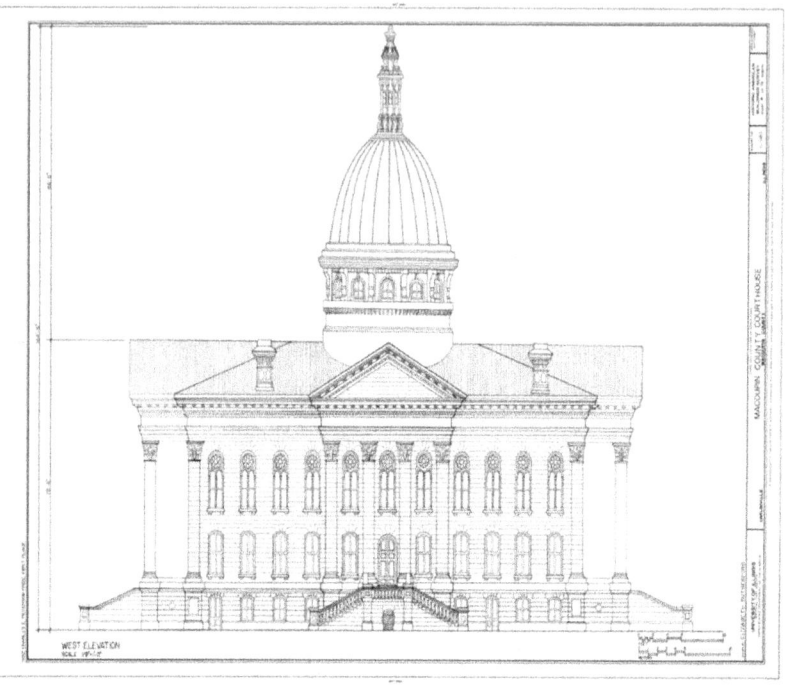

A BLUEPRINT OF THE COURTHOUSE DESIGN BY ELIJAH E. MYERS

there? Why did they need to hide it? The public had so many questions but very few answers.

By September 1867, with little more than the foundation underway, the new courthouse had already cost the taxpayers $13,000.00, not to mention the money already spent for the land. By the time the cornerstone was laid in October, the cost exceeded the $50,000 initial estimate. It was no secret that the cost of the new courthouse was going to greatly exceed the original amount obtained.

The Courthouse Committee continued to borrow money in the form of bonds. The bonds bore 10 percent interest, payable semi-annually, in many cases for a period of 10 years. The county was paying $100 over 10 years in interest. So, in a matter of 10 years, the county was really paying back $200 total on an original $100 bond. The county relied on citizens' taxes for repayment of these bonds, not to mention to payment for everything else the county needed to spend in order to function besides the courthouse construction.

ILLUSTRATION OF HOW THE FINISHED COURTHOUSE WAS INTENDED TO LOOK

As January 1869 rolled around, the cost had risen to an astounding $449,604.07 and an additional $125,000.00 was still required to complete the roof and magnificent dome. By now, the outrage against the Courthouse Committee was at an all-time high and on the verge of a riot. The county commissioners, low on funds and void of public support, were at a crossroads. They needed additional authorization through Illinois legislation to borrow even more money. They drafted legislation that would allow the county to borrow more funds, without a set limit. It would also allow a levy of an additional tax from year to year, not to exceed one percent, in addition to the taxes already secured on the bonds. Basically, they wanted to be able to spend whatever they wanted and increase the citizen's taxes to help pay off the bonds.

By February 23, 1869, the county commissioners' bill had passed the Senate but was still pending in the Illinois House. A group of 25 anti-Courthouse Committee citizens decided to head to Springfield in an attempt to persuade the House against the bill during the Judiciary Committee. Both sides were spirited in their pleas. The county commissioners admitted that plans for the building had been changed and in turn cost more than originally thought, but they assured the court that the building could be finished for less than $500,000. The citizens begged the State to stop the spending! They referred to the county commissioners as liars and thieves, who stole directly from the pockets of their citizens.

On March 3, 1869, the Judiciary Committee found in favor of the county commissioners. They reported that the increase in spending seemed to be from changing building plans, such as using iron and stone instead of wood and brick, which were used to quote the courthouse's original building price. Even though the spending was more than anticipated, the state found it was too late to stop building now and the bill allowing the continuation of construction and spending was passed. The legislation read as, "An Act to legalize certain acts of the county court of Macoupin County and to enable it to complete a court house in said county." Basically, the law allowed the county to complete the courthouse by any means the county determined. The support in favor of the bill from former Carlinville resident and now Illinois governor, John M. Palmer, who was discussed earlier in this book, was also a major motivator in the court's decision.

Macoupin County citizens were devastated that their government had let them down. However, they were ready to fight back and this time they would take it to the polls. In April 1869, the anti-Courthouse Committee began a slew of meetings aimed at shaking up local politics during the next election in November. Even though the citizens couldn't stop the county from spending or completing the courthouse, you bet they could vote those thieving officials out of office and that is exactly what they did. The Courthouse Committee members were not re-elected and new judges, Huggins, Atkins, and Olmstead were elected in their place. T. M. Metcalf replaced County Clerk George Holliday. As soon as the new men took office they made it their mission to get the courthouse completed. Disregarding all remaining plans, the men simply finished whatever was required to open the doors. The iron stairway to the dome, as well as the fourth-floor rooms, was never completed. Plans to include ornate statutes that to occupy the outside of the courthouse were ignored and all other finishing details were put off in order to save money.

EARLY 1900S POSTCARD DEPICTING THE FINISHED COURTHOUSE

When the building was finally completed in 1870 the bill was a whopping $1,342.000.00 which would be approximately $24 million in today's cash. For over a million dollars, the people of Macoupin County received a courthouse larger than the Illinois Statehouse and overall the second largest county courthouse in the entire country. While it may have not been the biggest, it was likely the most elaborate.

Even though not all the finishing touches were complete, the courthouse was a true gem that shined brightly. The interior and exterior walls are mostly limestone with additional stone, marble, and iron used inside. As you approach the building it's hard not to feel inferior. The Corinthian columns demand your respect and create a sense of awe and wonder. There are three completed floors in the courthouse including the basement area, which is where people

THE IMPRESSIVE COURTHOUSE COLUMNS

enter the building today. There is also a main floor and the upper floor, which houses an impressive court room. Rumors continue to persist that two tunnels exist under the courthouse, which are accessed through the basement area. The tunnels have been said to lead in two directions. One path leads to the county jail across the street and the other is believed to lead downtown to the Loomis House Hotel where it connects with another tunnel system running under the town square. If any tunnels once existed, they are inaccessible today.

The main courtroom on the upper floor features 4,500 square feet of space and room for around 600 people in the seats. It's reminiscent of the elaborate courtrooms seen in early cinema. You can even imagine Atticus Finch from *To Kill a Mockingbird* presenting his case in the historic court room. When completed, the main courtroom was adorned with a magnificent, and expensive, chandelier with 56 gas burners, which cost $3,000.

Over the years the outside of the dome has been painted a variety of colors including red and gold. A man named David Poole was granted the daring title of dome painter for the courthouse. Like a daredevil, David would dangle himself from the courthouse with a single rope tied around his waist. He had painted the courthouse six times before but was getting increasingly annoyed and worried about the number of wasps near the dome. He tied strings around his pant legs to try to keep the pesky insects out, hopefully avoiding stings. In 1945, he completed the paint job for the very last time, having avoided injury and serious stings each time. The courthouse that some dubbed as "cursed" allowed the painter to live to see another day. Ironically, the daring painter would die just two years after his last courthouse painting when he fell off a stepstool. Those who made it to the top of the dome were 191 feet off the ground. The towering dome even makes the courthouse visible from the outskirts of town.

The intricate features of the building are everywhere. Virtually all staircases, banisters, and doors are made out of iron and contain one-of-a-kind designs, including pelicans on a staircase banister, dog and wolf heads, flowers, foliage, and emblems. A lion's head with a door knocker in the center is featured on the main doors to the upper courtroom, giving an impressive knock against the iron door. Bronze sphinx were also featured on the chandeliers which hung throughout the building. One of the most impressive pieces of the courthouse was the judge's chair commissioned by Judge

COUNTY CLERK'S OFFICE IN 1912

Loomis. The chair is seven-feet-tall and made out of hand-carved walnut with lions carved into the armrests. It cost over $1,500 when it was completed in 1869. I don't know about you, but I can't even imagine spending $1,500 on a desk chair, let alone the $24,000 it would represent in today's cash. You can see how spending quickly got out of control. The features of the courthouse, while beautiful, were unnecessary and presented an attitude of wealth and prestige that sadly wasn't the reality of the county.

It took 32,000 citizens 40 years to pay off the debts left by the courthouse committee. On September 7, 1904 the town of Carlinville held a great celebration when the last of the bonds was paid off. Illinois Governor Charles Deneen publicly burned bond No. 720 at the jubilee with over 20,000 in attendance for the event.

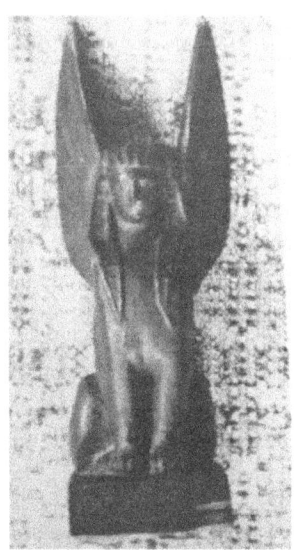

BRONX SPHINX THAT WAS ONCE DISPLAYED

THE JUDGE'S CHAIR HAS BEEN REPAIRED NUMEROUS TIMES WITH THE FIRST BEING IN 1925 BY THE CARLINVILLE WOMAN'S CLUB (SHOWN HERE)

The construction of the county courthouse led to an unprecedented rift between citizens and officials. Those in the community were unable to fully place their faith in officials, which led to Macoupin County adopting what was known as Township Government in 1871. Instead of appointing a centralized group of men to make county decisions, representatives from each township would form the county government.

Over the years there have been multiple theories about what or who caused the out of control budget that led to the Million Dollar Courthouse. Some say it was merely a miscalculation, albeit a very large miscalculation. Others are convinced something more deliberate and criminal occurred. The two men, Judge Loomis and County Clerk George Holliday, received the bulk of the blame. Judge Loomis' involvement as the lead courthouse commissioner left him vulnerable to culpability, as did the suspicious construction of his hotel, which many believed was paid for with courthouse funds. It was said that his over the top specifications for the courthouse, including the judge's chair that he requested, were overtly irresponsible. Once a respected judge, he would have very little time in the courthouse before being replaced by the voters in 1869. He was never formally accused of any wrongdoing, although the public would never allow him to restore his once fine reputation.

As far as George Holliday goes, he experienced a much different aftermath following the courthouse's completion. George Holliday was born August 5, 1824, in Kentucky. He was born into a large and religious family. His father, Reverend Charles Holliday, was a respected Methodist minister. In 1834, the Holliday family moved to the Macoupin County town of Chesterfield, a few miles outside of Carlinville. As a young man, George was well educated, graduating from McKendree College in Lebanon, Illinois. He

MACOUPIN COUNTY JUBILEE TO CELEBRATE THE LAST OF THE COURTHOUSE BONDS

spent his free time studying languages and science, as well as creating for himself a well-rounded resume of careers such as a surveyor, school commissioner, and, of course, county clerk. He also held positions in the newspaper industry as owner and editor of the *Carlinville Spectator*, a Democratic newspaper. As if his accomplishments weren't long enough, he also worked as the president of the Henderson Building and Loan Company. George and his wife, Cinderella, along with their six children, lived a privileged life in Carlinville. His wealth was without question, living in a prestigious house with one of the largest libraries in Illinois.

George Holliday's association with the Courthouse Committee changed his life forever. In 1868, he ended up selling the Carlinville newspaper. By this time, the public was unapologetically vocal about their dislike for the Courthouse Committee members and George's newspaper began to suffer. The reputation that he worked so hard to create was tarnished. When the courthouse opened in 1870, it was clear the citizens wanted someone to answer for the courthouse's price tag. George must have known trouble was headed his way because shortly after the courthouse completion, he quietly boarded a nightly Chicago and Alton train and left Carlinville, carrying only a carpet bag with him. He left his wife and children behind without so much as a "goodbye" or an explanation.

It seemed George's senses were correct. In 1871, he was indicted on 15 charges of larceny and embezzlement. Among the claims were accusations

GEORGE HOLLIDAY

that George knowingly signed his name to excessive orders and purchases that used the courthouse funds. He was the only one of the courthouse commissioners who faced criminal proceedings. In March 1872, Judge Arthur Gallagher presided in the absence of Judge Horatio Vandeveer, who was overseeing the case of *State v. Holliday*. Judge Gallagher had the charges against Holliday stricken from the docket with leave to reinstate if the State chose to do so. No further charges were ever brought and the county started to accept the idea that no one would be convicted of any wrongdoing in the courthouse matter.

Authorities did everything they could to spread the word about the missing former county clerk. A few days after his departure from Carlinville, former associates reported that George was spotted alive in New York City but any effort to retrieve the man was in vain. A week after his disappearance, another tip arrived. A body had been discovered in Niagara Falls. The body was of a man who resembled the general appearance of George Holliday but when relatives were contacted, and the body further examined, it was determined that it was not George after all. Reports of George sightings resembled that of Elvis sightings a few years ago. They were seeing him everywhere! An American traveler in South America said he was visiting a deserted convent when he found papers belonging to George Holliday. He said the papers were tax titles and were in George's handwriting. Verification of this information was never obtained.

A glimmer of hope for justice finally came a couple years after George's disappearance. A man named Samuel Hall was living in Olympia, Washington, and had a striking resemblance to Carlinville's own George Holliday. Authorities in Olympia determined that the man had only been living in Washington a couple of years and currently worked in the newspaper business, just like George had once done in Carlinville. Officials in Macoupin County thought it was worthwhile to send someone out to Washington to verify if the man known as Samuel Hall could in fact be George Holliday. Deputy Dan Delaney, who had once worked as a servant for the Holliday family, made the long journey out west. When he arrived, he sought out Samuel Hall and upon finding him, Sheriff Delaney immediately identified the man as George Holliday. The man from Washington denied the accusations but was still arrested and brought back to Carlinville. The town was in shock. They couldn't believe that they finally found George Holliday and could get some answers.

After the man arrived in town, Cinderella Holliday, George's wife, was brought to the jail to identify the man. Cinderella was unable to identify the man as her husband and the debate began. The town was yet again divided. Some were convinced the man was in fact George Holliday and others weren't so sure. The man, along with his attorney, immediately began *habeaus corpus* proceedings, seeking the man's release due to false identification. It was easy to see why someone may assume the man was George Holliday. They both were approximately the same age, same weight, same height, and same overall appearance. Unfortunately, forensics were a long way off and DNA testing was impossible.

The only way to settle the matter was to hold a hearing and have a judge decide if the man from Washington was George Holliday from Carlinville. The man from Washington was marched up the courtroom stairs and participated in one of the earliest and most notable hearings in the new courthouse. It seemed a bit ironic that the building which many considered an injustice to county citizens would be the place those same citizens hoped justice would finally be found.

Former friends and family of George Holliday took the stand to testify either in favor or against the idea that Samuel Hall was the missing man. The courtroom became eerily silent as they waited in anticipation for George's former dentist to testify. In front of the packed courtroom, the dentist examined the teeth of the man in question. With conviction, the dentist exclaimed that the gold teeth in the man's mouth matched the gold teeth that he had placed in George Holliday's mouth prior to his disappearance. The courtroom audience erupted with exclamations of joy that they finally had the evidence they needed.

Not so fast, though. The defense had their own star witness to call. Reverend Talbot, a minister from Washington who was said to know Samuel Hall, offered up some interesting information. The minister swore under oath that Samuel Hall was not George Holliday. In fact, the reverend testified that the man's real name was not even Samuel Hall. The courtroom let out a collective gasp. The state pushed the reverend to expose the man's true identity, but he declined to reveal any further information. The State objected to the reverend's refusal to cooperate, but the Judge allowed the reverend to remain quiet on the issue, stating that the court didn't need to know exactly

IDENTIFYING THE GOLD FILLED TEETH.

THE MAN'S TEETH ARE EXAMINED BY GEORGE HOLLIDAY'S DENTIST

who the man was, they just needed to know whether the man was George Holliday or not. Both sides rested their case and the judge deliberated. The final decision stated that there was not enough evidence to prove the man was George Holliday and he was to be released and sent back to Washington on the county's dime.

The man's attorney John Mayo Palmer, who was the son of the famous Carlinville resident General John Palmer, later revealed the man who called himself Samuel Hall was a former banker from Kentucky who was under investigation for brank fraud. His bank had failed and fearing retribution from locals, he ran away from Kentucky and ended up in Washington. Interestingly, after his return to Washington, "Hall" disappeared again. To this day, many people still believe that Hall was George Holliday – and that he escaped again. In 1878, Holliday was declared legally dead and his estate was settled. The remainder of his family moved to Missouri and never again heard from their missing husband and father.

The courthouse scandal is embedded in mysteries that we may never solve. Like many in the county, I believe embezzlement, as well as mismanagement of funds and overly extravagant design, created the Macoupin County's million-dollar mishap. I've heard theories that George Holliday was merely a pawn in an intricate scheme to fund the pockets of county officials. Those who believe that theory will say George hopped on that train in fear of his life after being threatened by the others involved. Personally, I don't believe George was innocent or dumb about what was happening. By all accounts, he was a highly intelligent and successful man who proved in the banking business that he knew how to handle money. I'm sure he also knew how to steal it, too. It was George's name that was signed numerous unapproved receipts that helped drive Macoupin County further into debt.

Now, I don't believe George acted alone. In fact, I speculate the scope of the fraudulent behavior goes beyond the Courthouse Committee. Even with the magnificence of the courthouse, the final price seemed unreasonable. A man named Charles Pond from St. Louis was brought in right before the courthouse opened to assess the value of the building. Under oath he stated that the final cost of the building should have been around $640,000. The actual cost was $700,000 more. In order to believe there wasn't any criminal activity involved with this discrepancy, you would have to believe the Courthouse Committee members, comprised entirely of successful business men, two of which were bankers, made major miscalculations and accounting errors over the entire course of the construction. I simply cannot bring myself to believe that.

Throughout the years, the Million Dollar Courthouse has continued to contain the secrets of its creation, as well as the energy of those who have come along since those early days. The building has housed not only an active county government and judicial system, but also other area businesses including the Carlinville Library, Macoupin County Agricultural Association, and offices of banker C. H. C Anderson. The history contained within the walls is extensive and if pay close attention, you may experience that history firsthand.

When I was 17-years-old I began a temporary internship in the Circuit Clerk's office housed at the courthouse. Overall it was a pleasant, easy-going job composed of filing, docket entry, and organization. At this time the courthouse was in the process of converting their records to electronic files.

AN EARLY PHOTOGRAPH OF THE MILLION DOLLAR COURTHOUSE. A BRIDGE CROSSING THE CARLINVILLE RIVER CAN BE SEEN TO THE RIGHT, AS WELL AS THE OLD JAIL.

As the intern, I was required to do the bulk of the grunt work, which included transporting files from place to place during the converting process. The dome houses the majority of the older records and I was asked from time to time to retrieve those documents. One hot summer day, I was up in the dome gathering files. The dome, while beautiful on the outside, was dusty and cluttered on the inside. As I was getting ready to carry a box of files downstairs, I heard footsteps coming towards me. I looked up and saw that no one was there. I paused for a second and then heard the footsteps again. The steps sounded like they belonged to someone wearing heavy boots. By this time, I realized I wasn't just hearing things and became a bit concerned. I quickly finished gathering what I needed and headed downstairs. To this day I have no explanation for the sound of those footsteps. That would be my first unexplained occurrence in the courthouse, but it wouldn't be my last.

It wasn't long after launching our *Haunted Carlinville* walking tours that I began to experience additional strange events in the building. During nights when we have a tour, I stop by the courthouse prior to beginning our night just to make sure the courthouse is ready for our group when we return later. One evening, I entered the building with a local Blackburn student who was assisting me on the tours. We entered on the basement level and as we walked towards the bathroom and vending machine area, we heard a giggle -- more specifically it sounded like the giggle of a girl. We both looked at each other as if to say, "do you hear what I hear?" We stood still, taking in all the sounds we possibly could. At that moment a shadow appeared to dart across the end of the hallway near where we entered. The shadow was dark and short, maybe about 3 feet tall. In that moment we were stunned. What had we just experienced?

During one of the early ghost hunts in the building, two separate groups of paranormal investigators experienced similar activity in a small courtroom near that hallway. One group reported communication with a spirit using a device that can obtain "yes" and "no" responses to questions. The device actually looks like a teddy bear. It contains EMF meters that will indicate EMF fluctuations by lighting up parts of the bear. The idea is that a spirit of a child may feel more comfortable communicating through a stuffed animal, rather than a plain EMF meter. The group explained that upon entering the courtroom they could feel the presence of a spirit. Through a series of questions and answers via the bear, they were able to ascertain that the spirit was a girl. The spirit reported feeling safe at the courthouse, which is why she still present in the building. They believed that an adoption might have something to do with her connection to the courthouse.

The same night another group approached me and also reported a spirit in the courtroom. They, too, felt the presence was of a girl and said they were also able to communicate with her through EMF responses. They specifically noted that she enjoyed having people visit her and liked playing games. After hearing their experiences, I had to wonder, was the giggle we heard that evening that of the girl's spirit? Maybe the shadow we saw was really just her way of playing a ghostly game of hide and seek.

The girl's spirit would resurface again, and this time it was through touch. At the end of our tour, the guests exit through the basement hallway. One evening, a couple of the ladies were getting drinks at the vending machine and freshening up before leaving. I was chatting with one of the women when out of nowhere she exclaims, "Who is that little girl?" She then pointed down the darkened hallway and explained that as she was chatting with me, she saw a little girl dart across the end of the hallway. She was

THE HALLWAY WHERE THE GHOSTLY GIGGLE WAS HEARD. THE SPIRIT OF THE GIRL IS OFTEN NOTICED IN THIS AREA

convinced that a young girl had gotten in the building. I walked with her over to the location of the sighting and looked around the courthouse but, of course, found nothing. I explained to her that we had recent reports of a girl's spirit near that hallway.

Later on that tour season, we had additional experiences with the girl in the hallway. I was leading a group out of the building when I heard one of the women behind me say, "Stop it!" I turned around and asked if everything was okay. She said that her friend had pulled on her shirt to scare her. Her friend swore she didn't pull on the woman's shirt. The woman explained that she felt someone tug on the bottom of her shirt, the way that a child might pull on your shirt to get attention. Like with the woman before, I shared with her the reports regarding the spirit of a young girl. The sensation of someone tugging on the bottom of a shirt continued to be reported every now and then for the rest of that tour season, and it was always reported by women.

One of the most intense interactions that I believe occurred with the girl's spirit took place in 2017, during a private tour. A group of senior citizens joined me in the courthouse for some haunted history and a miniature ghost hunt. We all gathered in the basement courtroom and experienced one of the longest conversations I believe I have ever observed with the other side. While in the courtroom, I began to share the paranormal experiences involving the girl. We had several EMF meters present, as well as several individuals holding dowsing rods. It didn't take long for an EMF meter near the witness chair to light up. I asked, "if any spirit is present to please light up the meter again." On cue, the meter lit up. I then asked for it to back away from the meter to stop the lights. Again, the meter obliged. At this point, I assured whatever was present that we were there as friends and were only wanting to communicate with them. I asked for the spirit to show us a "yes" response by lighting up the meter lights and a "no" response by leaving the lights off.

Again, I asked if anyone was present to which I received a "yes." Through a series of questions and responses, we were able to conclude that we were talking to young pre-teen girl. Her story was a sad one, she was abused by a father figure and spent a considerable amount of time at the courthouse because of the abuse. I was blown away not only by the consistent responses through the EMF meter but also the corresponding responses by the dowsing rods. The group in the courtroom consisted of mostly women, to which I must say all of whom showed incredible love and compassion for the girl. They even took over asking the questions and held a conversation with the spirit for 15 solid minutes. Sometimes she was hesitant to give us information but, overall, she was very responsive. We were able to obtain incredible personal information and unlock some of the girl's past. I think that was only possible because of the women in that room. We all felt the girl's presence during the conversation and just as quickly as she appeared, we all felt her start to fade. We thanked her and said goodbye, with some of the women offering grandmotherly words or encouragement and wisdom to the spirit. It was a truly incredibly and unique experience that I will always remember.

There is another spirit that is felt in the basement area courtroom and this one is believed to be male. This spirit may be the cause of an unpleasant feeling that several have experienced. There are two locations in the courtroom that have caused people, mostly men, physical pain and discomfort. Near the judge's chair several have reported the feeling of a tight chest; when they exit the room the feeling disappears. A similar feeling along with stomach and head pain has been felt near the back window. Several groups have obtained communication with this spirit through EMF meter responses and dowsing rods which have revealed the spirit's gender as male and as having a connection to the building at his time of death. The spirit does not seem to be causing the discomfort out of animosity but rather as a way to show his presence and tell the story of his pain. During a communication session with what we believe was this particular male spirit, it was revealed that he was involved in law enforcement.

While not all hauntings have a documented history to support their existence, I think it's important to explore the history of a location to better gain a perspective on the energy surrounding it. Based on age alone, the courthouse is bound to have some tragic events occur on the grounds. These events may or may not fuel the hauntings inside, but either way I think they are important to remember and respect. I can't be certain of the identity of the male spirit, but I did uncover some interesting history.

WILLIAM FISHBACK

On August 25, 1872, Macoupin County Sheriff, William Fishback had a normal start to his morning. He ate a nice breakfast, shaved, and put on a clean shirt. He seemed to be in good spirits as he headed to his office, located in the courthouse. On his way he saw a few friends and joked around a bit, even offering a cheerful smile to those he passed. He entered his office and took off his hat, placing it on the table. He then removed his coat and vest, folding them up and placing them next to his hat. Next, William gathered a stack of 10 or 12 letters and placed them carefully and purposefully in his hat. William pulled out his office chair and took a seat, slowly leaning it back until his head reached the iron arrow railing. With deliberation, the sheriff then placed a revolver to his right temple and pulled the trigger. The sound of the gun echoed throughout the building. A lawyer in an adjoining office rushed to see what had happened. He discovered the lifeless body of William Fishback along with a letter on the desk. The letter read, "Farwell [sic], wife and children. Forgive me, but I must leave you."

The contents of the letters that were placed in the hat are unknown but the dates on the envelope were reported to range from August 12 to August 24. Local newspapers reported that Sheriff Fishback was a highly-respected member of Macoupin County. It was assumed the he would have served another term as Sheriff, having gained the confidence of the citizens. No specific reason was released concerning the reason for suicide.

Further evidence would be provided to support this male spirit by fellow American Hauntings guide and investigator Luke Naliborski. While in the courtroom, he was investigating using a digital recorder. When he asked if the spirit present worked at the courthouse, he recorded an EVP that responded with a gentle "yes." Two words also emerged: "policeman" and "hurt."

Other information that night was provided with the help of Luke and another American Hauntings alum, Len Adams. After investigating for some time, one group decided to participate in a spirit box session. The spirit box is a device that used radio frequencies and is believed to assist entities with communication. Several times during the night, it sounded like someone was saying "hello" through the static. Even more clear was the name "Lauren." This was heard after asking the name of the spirit we were communicating with.

On a separate occasion, a very interesting dowsing rod session took place. Through a serious of responses indicating "yes" and "no", whoever was communicating revealed that there were six spirits in the courthouse, including s young girl and Judge Loomis himself.

Judge Loomis' spirit has also been reported at his hotel on the square. I'm by no means a paranormal expert, but in the realm of the unexplained I'm sure it's possible to haunt two places. I mean, why not? In my opinion, Judge Loomis is the top candidate for the courthouse hauntings. Think about it, Judge Loomis prided himself on his position as county judge. We can see his pride by the obscenely expensive Judge's throne he had made. He had every intention of not only remaining on the bench after the courthouse was completed but doing so like a king. When he lost the election and was removed as judge, he lost his place in local society along with his respect in the community. It was Judge Loomis who was given the most power in the courthouse construction and he was never able to fully enjoy its glory.

THE JUDGE'S BENCH TODAY

One of the most frightening experiences to happen in the courthouse is thought to have been caused by Judge Loomis' ghost. During our tours of the courthouse, I ask the person helping me to go upstairs and turn on the lights of the upper courtroom, so the tour group can take pictures of the beautiful features. One particular recruit had completed this task several times before but this night something was different. She headed upstairs and, within a minute or two, I heard this horrifying scream. I then saw her bolt down the stairs to rejoin our group. I asked her what happened, and she explained that someone, or something, was upstairs. Still shaking, she said that as she approached the door to open the courtroom she looked off to her left, which is near the entry way of the jury room, and thought she saw a tall dark shadow standing in the doorway. She told herself it must be her imagination and she stepped forward towards the courtroom door. As she grabbed the doorknob to open it, she felt someone step out from the jury room and grab her backpack, pulling her away from the door. That was when she screamed and hurried downstairs. She vowed to never go up in the courtroom alone again. After hearing her story, I can't help but feel it was Judge Loomis who pulled her back, as if to say, "Don't go in my courtroom."

I feel as though the upper courtroom is the most likely spot to find Judge Loomis. His hand-carved judge's chair still sits front and center, as if it is watching over the courtroom. During the tours, we shut off all the lights in the courtroom and guests take a seat either in the pews or the jury area. My back is always to the judge's area and facing those in the audience. As I tell the stories of the courthouse scandal, as well as some of the court cases that have come in and out of the courtroom, I can feel someone watching me from behind. In the darkness I can't decipher any specific shapes or forms of what may be peering at me, but I can tell they are present. I'm led to believe it may be Judge Loomis who is watching. I don't feel threatened by whatever is joining us on the tour. Instead, I feel as though whatever is there is just observing. One night, as I was getting ready to finish my stories in the courtroom, I heard someone begin to cry and become upset. I remembered that a young boy was on my tour that night, so I stopped what I was doing to make sure he was okay and turn on the lights, if needed. The mother insisted that I finish my story and assured me her son was just fine. At the end of the tour, I asked the mother what happened. She said that during my stories her son looked out the window of the courthouse door towards the hallway where an emergency light. When he looked up he saw a dark figure of a man staring in the window.

Another reason I am led to believe that Judge Loomis may be haunting the courthouse is based on a certain topic that tends to yield paranormal responses. Several investigators have reported that speaking of Judge Loomis' family history – specifically about the so-called Loomis gang -- will cause unexplained noises such as footsteps in the courtroom, as well as unusual shadows to appear. I'm not a fan of antagonizing the dead but I do find it interesting that this topic creates an increase in activity.

Other interesting paranormal occurrence in the courtroom concerns the iron doors. Each door that opens to the courtroom is made of solid iron and weighs over one ton. There is no way to open these doors without using some sort of physical force. During the course of investigating the courthouse, there have been at least two separate occasions where people have witnessed the massive doors opening on their own. No draft or breeze could possibly cause

THE HEAVY IRON DOORS IN THE COURTROOM

the doors to move. Whatever caused the doors to open must have had a strong presence.

The courtroom is also known to be an excellent place to take photographs. Not only is the room architecturally interesting, but unusual anomalies have been known to show up in pictures. One particular group was taking photos around the judge's bench. Upon review of the photo they saw

THE IRON RAILINGS ARE ORIGINAL TO THE COURTHOUSE

what appeared to be the head of a man floating in mid-air. The head wasn't as solid as you would expect a living human's head to appear, but the shape and features of the face were apparent. Others have noted similar photos where they see people's faces or even full bodies outlined on their photos. Photography can be an amazing tool when it comes to capturing the paranormal. However, it's important to keep in mind that reflections, lighting, and natural shadows can cause odd objects to appear in photos. Even so, the photos captured in this area are interesting and are worthy of discussion.

The second floor of the building isn't without its share of hauntings, specifically with objects. It should be noted that the second floor houses a control room with more electronics than one person can count. You will see spikes in EMF near this location that are completely normal. However, there are some unusual EMF spikes that have consistently occurred. In recent years, several military uniforms have been placed on display on the second floor. Without fail, people have consistently reported feeling an energy surrounding this area. They have also noted high EMF readings in this location. The uniforms are located near the elevator, which I had assumed was the cause of the high EMF. Although, when you place the EMF meter against the wall, or even point it in the direction of the elevator, the EMF is low. But when you place it near this one particular uniform, the EMF increases. Down the hallway of the second floor, you will find a row of wooden chairs. For whatever reason, there is one particular chair that will always emit high EMF readings. Several people have inspected the chair to see if it has some sort of electrical device underneath it or anything attached that would cause the high EMF, but nothing has ever been found. It also doesn't seem to matter where the chair is placed. No matter where the chair is located, the EMF around it is high. It's always fun to see those on the tour find the mysterious chair and get their perspective on the situation.

ONE OF THE GORGEOUS STAIRCASES ON THE SECOND FLOOR

The courthouse is not only an active paranormal location, but it is still an active courthouse. Countless people have come through the doors over the years, many of whom have experienced life-changing events within its walls. The courthouse has been filled with joyous events including weddings, adoptions, and home purchases. It has also been filled with devastation. Divorce, restraining orders, civil proceedings, and even murder trials have been a constant presence. It's not surprising that the energy of those impactful moments still resonates in the building.

The Million Dollar Courthouse remains a testimony to local greed, deceit, and misfortune, but despite that sordid reputation, the courthouse also stands as a reminder of local resilience and triumph displayed by those who so vocally demanded respect and representation from their county officials. The building's beauty and strength still gets people talking and remains a popular stop for out of town visitors.

If the Macoupin County Courthouse has taught me anything, it's that history, while thought of as our past, can be very much alive in our future. I'm reminded of the expression, "if walls could talk." I don't know if the Million Dollar Courthouse would give up all its secrets, but if you listen closely, you may hear it whisper.

AFTERWORD

The history and hauntings of Carlinville and Macoupin County proves that even in small rural towns there are secrets to uncover and spirits to reveal. During my last four years of haunted research and conducting tours in Carlinville, I have been constantly amazed by the amount of people who approach me with their own stories of hauntings and family history. For those of you who shared your stories with me, I am grateful.

Completing this book has been a long journey for me. When I think about it, there have been numerous events that seemed irrelevant but have led up to where I am today. In fact, this journey started about 20 years ago with a phantom knock on my door.

I spent my childhood in the small Macoupin County town of Medora. When I say "small" I mean *small*. There were only 500 citizens in our community with one gas station and one grocery store providing you with the bulk of your entertainment. I lived in an early 1900s era craftsman-style home on Locust Street that my parents spent countless hours renovating over the years. For as long as I can remember, I knew my house was special. I imagine all kids think that to a certain degree, but my house had a very particular personality.

Doors would open by themselves, voices were heard when you were all alone, and objects had a way of moving with no human hand guiding them. For years, I was terrified to sleep in my room. I would even drag my blankets out to the hallway and sleep on the floor just to avoid being alone in my bedroom. I was convinced someone, or something, was watching me.

They say you can grow accustomed to almost anything and that's exactly what happened. There came a point where the strange noises and unexplained events became normal and they no longer upset me the way they once did. They became so normal in fact, that I began to stop noticing them altogether. That is until one day when I was about 12 years-old. I was sitting in my bedroom when, out of nowhere, there was a knock on the door. I shouted "come in" thinking it must have been one of my parents knocking. I waited for the door knob to turn but nothing happened. I heard the knock again. I shouted, "come in" and still the door remained closed. I jumped up from my bed and opened the door, expecting to find my mom or dad, the only other people in the house, on the other side. There was no one. I was old enough to think of a logical explanation and assumed it was a draft pulling on the door causing it to make a knocking sound. Within a week, the knocking happened again, then again, and again, until the knocking on my door was accompanied by something more disturbing. Whatever was knocking was now saying my name.

After realizing the knocking and voice was not from a living person in the home, I had to admit to myself that something unexplainable was occurring. On a semi-regular basis for the next six years, there would be a knock on my door, sometimes followed by what sounded like someone shouting my name from a distance. The knocking eventually became routine and I chalked it up to another interesting personality trait of my home. One day out of curiosity, I knocked back at whatever was at my door. It responded with a similar knock and I decided that was enough experimentation for the day. On days when the knocking would become annoying, I would generally shout out loud, "leave me alone" or "stop bothering me, I'm busy" as if I was yelling at an annoying younger sibling. The house would always listen and leave me to whatever task I was trying to complete.

My parents and I moved out of the house when I was 18. It was one of the saddest goodbyes I ever experienced. While there were aspects of the home that were unnerving, I had fallen in love with its character and its spirit. After leaving that home I never again experienced the knocking that occurred throughout my childhood and I must admit, I sometimes miss it.

For many years, I was careful as to who I told about my childhood haunted house. Some people will assume you're crazy or you watch too many horror films. I'm telling this story now because I realize that without that haunted house, and without that knocking, I never would have opened my mind to the possibilities of something outside my own reality. I never would have planned a paranormal investigation that eventually led to a job with American Hauntings. I never would have organized or written the *Haunted Carlinville Tour*, and I never would have written this book.

Looking back, I'm thankful for those fearful sleepless nights, strange noises, and the haunted history of my family home. I know now that whenever the strange and unusual comes knocking, I will answer.

"To learn what we fear is to learn who we are. Horror defies our boundaries and illuminates our souls."
-Shirley Jackson, *The Haunting of Hill House*

BIBLIOGRAPHY

History of Madison County, Illinois, Illustrated with Biographical Sketches of Many Prominent Men and Pioneers, 1882
Macoupin County Courthouse Centennial, 1867
Palmer, John. *Personal Recollections of John M. Palmer, The Story of an Earnest Life*, 1901
Portrait and Biographical Album of Macoupin County, Illinois, 1891
Taylor, Troy. *Ghosts of the Prairie*, 2016
Walker, Charles A. *History of Macoupin County Illinois, Biographical and Pictorial*, 1911

NEWSPAPERS:

Ashton Gazette
Alton Telegraph
Cairo Bulletin
Carlinville Democrat
Carlinville Spectator
Chicago Inter-Ocean
Chicago Tribune
Daily Independent
Decatur Daily Herald
Decatur Daily Republican
Decatur Daily Review
Edwardsville Intelligencer
Gillespie News
Jacksonville Daily Journal
Jefferson City Post-Tribune
Journal Gazette
Macoupin County Enquirer-Democrat
Nebraska Advertiser
The Pantograph

St. Louis Globe
St. Louis Post-Dispatch
State Journal Register
Topeka State Journal

Personal interviews, correspondence, and public forums.

SPECIAL THANKS TO:
Lois Taylor and Lisa Taylor Horton: Editing
April Slaughter: Cover Design and Artwork
Troy Taylor: Layout and Design
Macoupin County Sheriff's Office and County Board
Len Adams
Sarah Anna Anderson
Jennifer Reid Baugher
Robert Brown
Courtney Egner
Stacy Gross
Dawn Helm
Hollywood & Vine
Madison "Mad" Jones
Macoupin County Enquirer-Democrat Newspaper
Luke Naliborski
Sonny & Susie Schardan
Dakota Tebbe
John Winterbauer
And everyone who has joined me on a *Haunted Carlinville Tour* or shared a story with me. Thank you!

Note: Although American Hauntings Ink, Kaylan Schardan and all affiliated with this book have carefully researched all sources to insure the accuracy and completeness of all information contained here, we assume no responsibility for errors, inaccuracies, or omissions

www.ingramcontent.com/pod-product-compliance
Lightning Source LLC
LaVergne TN
LVHW021119080426
835510LV00012B/1753